SENSING GOD
GARY HOLLOWAY

21st Century Christian

Sensing God
ISBN: 978-0-89098-951-7

©2025 by 21st Century Christian, Inc
Nashville, TN 37215
All rights reserved.

All rights reserved. No part of this publication may be reproduced, stored in a retrieval system, or transmitted in any form or by any means—electronic, mechanical, photocopy, recording, digital, or otherwise—without the written permission of the publisher.

Unless otherwise indicated, all Scripture quotations are taken from the Holy Bible, New Living Translation, copyright © 1996, 2004, 2015 by Tyndale House Foundation. Used by permission of Tyndale House Publishers, Carol Stream, Illinois 60188. All rights reserved.

Scripture quotations marked (NIV) are taken from the Holy Bible, New International Version®, NIV®. Copyright © 1973, 1978, 1984, 2011 by Biblica, Inc.® Used by permission of Zondervan. All rights reserved worldwide. www.zondervan.com The "NIV" and "New International Version" are trademarks registered in the United States Patent and Trademark Office by Biblica, Inc.®

Scripture quotations marked (GNT) are from the Good News Translation in Today's English Version – Second Edition Copyright © 1992 by American Bible Society. Used by Permission.

Cover design by Jared Kendall

Dedication

To Adam and Abbie Graham,
who are leading a new generation to experience God

CONTENTS

INTRODUCTION 7

1 SEEING GOD 11
Exodus 19:16-21, Exodus 33:18-23, Genesis 32:24-30, Job 19:25-27, Revelation 22:1-5

2 SEEING JESUS 21
Luke 2:15-18, 25-32; Matthew 2:9-11, John 14:8-10, 20:24-29; Hebrews 12:1-2, Revelation 1:7

3 TASTING GOD 31
Genesis 2:7-9, Exodus 24:9-11, Deuteronomy 8:2-3, Isaiah 25:6, 55:1-2

4 TASTING JESUS 41
John 2:9-10, John 6:35, 47-58; 1 Corinthians 10:16-18, Revelation 19:6-9

5 SMELLING GOD 51
Genesis 8:20-21, Psalm 45:6-8, 115:4-6; Isaiah 1:13, 65:1-5; Romans 12:1, 2 Corinthians 2:14-16, Hebrews 13:15-16

6 SMELLING JESUS 59
Luke 7:36-48, John 19:38-42, Ephesians 5:1-2

7 TOUCHING GOD 69
Exodus 19:11-12, 2 Samuel 6:3-7, Isaiah 6:1-8, 41:10-13; Hosea 11:3-4

8 TOUCHING JESUS 77
Matthew 17:5-8, 19:13-15; Mark 5:24-34, 40-42; Luke 7:14-15, John 20:26-29, 1 John 1:1

9 HEARING GOD 87
Genesis 2:15-17, Exodus 3:4-10, Deuteronomy 6:1-9, 1 Samuel 3:1-10, Isaiah 30:19-21

10 HEARING JESUS **97**
Matthew 7:24-27, 13:10-13; John 4:39-42, 5:28-29, 10:24-27;
1 John 5:13-15

11 SENSING THE FATHER **107**
Psalm 8:3-5, 19:1-4; Matthew 5:14-16, Romans 1:19-20,
2 Timothy 3:15-17, Hebrews 4:12-13, 1 John 4:20-21

12 SENSING THE SON. **117**
John 14:13-14, 16:23-24; Romans 6:3-5, 8:34; Galatians 3:26-28,
Hebrews 7:24-25, 10:19-22; 1 John 2:1, 3:2; Colossians 3:4

13 SENSING THE SPIRIT **127**
Joel 2:28-29, John 14:17-18, 23; Romans 15:16, Galatians 5:22-25,
1 Corinthians 2:13-14, 6:19-20; 1 Peter 1:2, 2 Peter 1:20-21

INTRODUCTION

This is an invitation to experience God — Father, Son, and Spirit.

How do we make sense of the Trinity?

It's a question that has challenged Christians since the beginning of the church. For several centuries, Christian leaders debated what it meant to confess there is one God and still believe in Father, Son, and Spirit. They disagreed on the importance of the doctrine. After much time, councils of Christian scholars and leaders produced confessions and definitions that they thought clarified the doctrine of the Trinity, but they could not fully agree.

Even today, the idea of the Trinity baffles many Christians. Others simply try not to think about it. Some even outright reject the teaching.

Why do Christians believe in the Trinity anyway? We believe in one God. Isn't that enough? Where did the idea originate?

It came from the experience of the earliest disciples who saw Jesus in the flesh. After being with Him for a few years, and particularly after His resurrection, they came to believe that He was the Word made flesh (John 1:14). One disciple calls Him, "My Lord and my God" (John 20:28). Others say He created everything (Colossians 1:16). Those who said this were devout Jews who passionately believed there was one God. They did not think of Jesus as a second God, but as the same God who made the world, called Abraham, led Israel out of slavery, and gave them His instruction. They confessed one God but also spoke of Father and Son.

Then there is the Spirit. The Old Testament speaks of the Holy Spirit, but it was Jesus who spoke of Him as a person who would live in His followers. Jesus says He would continue to be with His disciples through the Spirit (John 14:15-26). One God — Father, Son, Spirit.

So, are you now clear on the Trinity? Probably not. The Bible speaks of Father, Son, and Spirit but does not clearly explain the relation among them. For centuries, thoughtful Christians have tried to clarify that relationship. They have not completely succeeded. Why not? Because we are talking of the God who is beyond our imagination. God will always be a mystery. The Trinity will always be a mystery. This is not a way of avoiding difficult thought about the Trinity, but rather is a confession of faith in a God we cannot fathom.

How do we make sense of the Trinity?

We can't. We can, however, experience God, Father, Son, and Spirit through our senses. This book takes another approach to making "sense" of the Trinity. We perceive reality through our five senses — sight, smell, taste, touch, and hearing. God made us that way. We also use those senses to encounter the living

God. Because Jesus had a human body, He also had those senses. We sense Jesus. He senses us. What's more, the Bible speaks of God the Father in terms of the senses. The Father senses us. We sense the Father. The same is true of the Spirit.

As we explore the language of the five senses in the Bible, we will intimately experience our relationship with the one triune God. God invites us to go beyond understanding the Trinity. He invites us to enter His life.

ONE
SEEING GOD

Exodus 19:16-21, Exodus 33:18-23, Genesis 32:24-30, Job 19:25-27, Revelation 22:1-5

There's an enormous difference between description and seeing. That's true with people. Someone describes their friend that you've never seen as "average height, brown hair, blue eyes, and a little on the hefty side." You have a picture of him in your mind. Then you meet him face to face and think, *That's not how I pictured him at all.*

It works that way with places, too. I like to travel. I plan my trips by looking at photos, rankings, and maps of where I am going. When I get there, it never quite looks like the pictures. Maps also deceive me. Looking at the map I think, *I can easily walk that*, only to find when I arrive that the entire journey is uphill. Descriptions, photos, and maps don't lie, they just are not the same as seeing for yourself.

Then there are those sights that we cannot fully see. I recently made my fourth trip to the Grand Canyon. No photo or painting

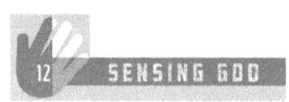

can do justice to its beauty. Even when you see it with your own eyes, the scene changes with almost every step. Have I seen the Grand Canyon? Yes and no. No one has fully seen it.

It's the same way with God. We want to see God. We long to be with Him face to face. We want to catch a glimpse of His majesty, power, and love.

Can we?

NO ONE CAN SEE GOD

The Bible clearly says that no one can see God.

After God delivers Israel from slavery in Egypt, He leads them to Mount Sinai. There, He appears to them but gives a strict warning.

> On the morning of the third day, thunder roared and lightning flashed, and a dense cloud came down on the mountain. There was a long, loud blast from a ram's horn, and all the people trembled. Moses led them out from the camp to meet with God, and they stood at the foot of the mountain. All of Mount Sinai was covered with smoke because the LORD had descended on it in the form of fire. The smoke billowed into the sky like smoke from a brick kiln, and the whole mountain shook violently. As the blast of the ram's horn grew louder and louder, Moses spoke, and God thundered his reply. The LORD came down on the top of Mount Sinai and called Moses to the top of the mountain. So Moses climbed the mountain.
>
> Then the LORD told Moses, "Go back down and warn the people not to break through the boundaries to see the LORD, or they will die."
>
> EXODUS 19:16-21

God's people saw unmistakable evidence of His presence — thunder, lightning, cloud, and smoke — but they could not see God and live.

While Moses is on the mountain receiving the Lord's instruction for Israel, the people grow tired of waiting and demand that Aaron make a god for them that they can see. He fashions a golden calf, which they worship. The Lord is so angry at this rejection of His covenant that He threatens to destroy them. Moses intercedes for Israel. The Lord does not destroy them, but He says, "But I will not travel among you, for you are a stubborn and rebellious people. If I did, I would surely destroy you along the way" (Exodus 33:3). Moses convinces God to go with them and asks to see God. God tells him, "But you may not look directly at my face, for no one may see me and live" (Exodus 33:20).

The New Testament also teaches that no one can see God. "No one has ever seen God" (1 John 4:12). God "lives in light so brilliant that no human can approach him. No human eye has ever seen him, nor ever will" (1 Timothy 6:16).

WHY CAN'T WE SEE GOD?

Why does God not allow us to see Him? Does He not want us to see Him? Is God hiding from us?

No. We humans simply do not have the capacity to see God. It's like looking directly into the sun. The brilliance of God's glory will blind us, even kill us. In the Bible, when angels come from the presence of God to speak to humans, their first words are often, "Don't be afraid" (see Genesis 21:17, Daniel 10:12, Matthew 28:5, Luke 1:30, Acts 27:24). When one sees an angel, they react with terror because those angels come from the presence of the Almighty God. To see God face to face would frighten us to death.

We sometimes say, "I see," when we mean, "I understand." When the Bible says we cannot see God, it means He is beyond all human understanding. In the words of the fourth-century theologian, Augustine of Hippo, "If you understood him, it would not be God." This may be one of the reasons God forbids images. Israel is rightly too afraid to see God, but they want a "god" they can see. Humans make images and can manipulate those "gods." We cannot control the only true God. We can only fall face down in reverence of His power and holiness.

SOME WHO SAW GOD

The Bible also has stories of those who saw God and lived to tell about it. Even though God warned Moses that he could not see His face, God still appears to Moses.

> Moses responded, "Then show me your glorious presence."
> The LORD replied, "I will make all my goodness pass before you, and I will call out my name, Yahweh, before you. For I will show mercy to anyone I choose, and I will show compassion to anyone I choose. But you may not look directly at my face, for no one may see me and live." The LORD continued, "Look, stand near me on this rock. As my glorious presence passes by, I will hide you in the crevice of the rock and cover you with my hand until I have passed by. Then I will remove my hand and let you see me from behind. But my face will not be seen."
>
> EXODUS 33:18-23

Moses cannot see the face of God, but he does see the back of God's glorious presence.

However, there are other times when Moses sees the Lord "face to face" (Deuteronomy 34:10). Moses even says Israel saw God's face at Sinai, "At the mountain the LORD spoke to you face to face from the heart of the fire" (Deuteronomy 5:4).

Earlier, Jacob had a face-to-face encounter with the Lord.

> This left Jacob all alone in the camp, and a man came and wrestled with him until the dawn began to break. When the man saw that he would not win the match, he touched Jacob's hip and wrenched it out of its socket. Then the man said, "Let me go, for the dawn is breaking!"
>
> But Jacob said, "I will not let you go unless you bless me."
>
> "What is your name?" the man asked.
>
> He replied, "Jacob."
>
> "Your name will no longer be Jacob," the man told him. "From now on you will be called Israel, because you have fought with God and with men and have won."
>
> "Please tell me your name," Jacob said.
>
> "Why do you want to know my name?" the man replied. Then he blessed Jacob there.
>
> Jacob named the place Peniel (which means "face of God"), for he said, "I have seen God face to face, yet my life has been spared."
>
> GENESIS 32:24-30

Jacob encounters a stranger, wrestles with him until dawn, and will not let go of him before he receives a blessing. After this experience, Jacob is sure it was the Lord who wrestled with him, God in human form, a preview of things to come. He had seen the face of God. Seeing God is not easy. It requires that we do not let go of God when we wrestle with who He is and what He does. If you cannot see God, do not give up.

No one can see God and live. Jacob, Moses, and Israel saw the face of God and lived. These teachings are in the Bible. How can both be true?

Perhaps the key is in the Moses story in Exodus 33. Moses does not see God's self, His essence. No one can fully comprehend God. What God reveals to Moses is His goodness and His glory. Humans cannot see the totality of the Lord. If we tried, our minds and hearts would burst like a balloon with too much air. What God will do at times is reveal His glory in a vision.

Micaiah the prophet says, "I saw the LORD sitting on his throne with all the armies of heaven around him, on his right and on his left" (1 Kings 22:19). Isaiah says, "It was in the year King Uzziah died that I saw the Lord. He was sitting on a lofty throne, and the train of his robe filled the Temple" (Isaiah 6:1). Amos says, "Then he showed me another vision. I saw the Lord standing beside a wall that had been built using a plumb line" (Amos 7:7).

These prophets and others have clear visions of the Lord. Jacob's vision is more than visual. He wrestles with God. Moses has so many visions of God that we can say he saw Him "face to face." Yet it is not God Himself they see. It is a manifestation of His glory.

WHAT IT TAKES TO SEE GOD

What about us who are not prophets and do not have visions. Can we see God?

Yes! What does it take to see God?

It takes great faith. We have to trust that God will appear to us, especially when we cannot see Him in our lives. When it looks like God has abandoned us, still we trust that we will see our Redeemer with our own eyes. If there is one person in the Bible who did not see God in his life, it was Job. God allows Satan to kill Job's family and to destroy Job's health. Job's wife and friends turn against him. Job cries out to God and asks, "Why?" He gets no answer. Yet Job will not give up on the Lord.

> "But as for me, I know that my Redeemer lives,
>   and he will stand upon the earth at last.
> And after my body has decayed,
>   yet in my body I will see God!
> I will see him for myself.
> Yes, I will see him with my own eyes.
> I am overwhelmed at the thought!"
>
> JOB 19:25-27

These verses in Hebrew are notoriously difficult to translate and raise many questions. Scholars disagree on their meaning. Does the "redeemer" refer to God? Does Job expect to see the Lord in this life or after death? In his current body or a resurrected body? I do not have all the answers to those questions, but Christian readers of Job have for centuries understood these words as amazing words of faith. Though the Old Testament does not have a clear teaching on the afterlife and resurrection, Job trusts that God will make things right in his life. If he does not see God now, he believes he will see Him in a new body with new eyes.

And Job does see God in this life. The Lord appears to him in a whirlwind (Job 38:1). After that Job says, "I had only heard about you before, but now I have seen you with my own eyes" (Job 42:5).

What did it take for Job to see God? Amazing trust and suffering. Job underwent a series of terrible ordeals before seeing

God. Jacob also had a sore hip the rest of his life following his sighting of the Lord. It takes faith to see God. Suffering faith.

What's more, it takes a pure heart to see God. Jesus says, "God blesses those whose hearts are pure, for they will see God" (Matthew 5:8). What is purity of heart? It means we desire only one thing — to see God. Just as a glass of pure water contains nothing but water with no impurities, so our hearts are to contain nothing but God. The psalmist puts it this way, "Because I am righteous, I will see you. When I awake, I will see you face to face and be satisfied" (Psalm 17:15). We must want to see God more than we want anything else. This is why the Bible warns of having a divided heart or mind. "Come close to God, and God will come close to you. Wash your hands, you sinners; purify your hearts, for your loyalty is divided between God and the world (James 4:8).

A suffering trust from a pure heart. That's what it takes to see God.

THE BEATIFIC VISION

We see God in many ways each day. We see Him in the beauty of creation. We see His powerful acts of blessing. We see Him in family and friends. We see Him in Scripture.

But the day will come when we see God face to face. The Lord will show us the fullness of his glory. "For now we see only a reflection as in a mirror; then we shall see face to face" (1 Corinthians 13:12, NIV).

That complete vision of God only comes after our resurrection. The Lord will return, bringing a new heaven and earth. With it, He will raise our bodies with new eyes to see clearly what we could not see before. Some Christians refer to this as the beatific vision, the sight not just of the beauty of creation but of the One who is Beauty itself.

> Then the angel showed me a river with the water of life, clear as crystal, flowing from the throne of God and of the Lamb. It flowed down the center of the main street. On each side of the river grew a tree of life, bearing twelve crops of fruit, with a fresh crop each month. The leaves were used for medicine to heal the nations.
>
> No longer will there be a curse upon anything. For the throne of God and of the Lamb will be there, and his servants will worship him. And they will see his face, and his name will be written on their foreheads. And there will be no night there — no need for lamps or sun — for the Lord God will shine on them. And they will reign forever and ever.
>
> REVELATION 22:1-5

The day will come when the most beautiful sight we have ever seen will pale in comparison with the glorious face of God. May that day come quickly!

QUESTIONS FOR REFLECTION

1. Do you want to see God? Why?

2. Why does the Bible say no one can see God?

3. Why does God show Himself to certain people in the Bible?

4. How does God show Himself to certain people in the Bible?

5. What does it take to see God?

6. Imagine what it will be like to see God in the new heaven and earth. How will God look?

SEEING JESUS

Luke 2:15-18, 25-32, Matthew 2:9-11, John 14:8-10, 20:24-29, Hebrews 12:1-2, Revelation 1:7

Friends know I travel, so they sometimes ask me, "What is the most awe-inspiring sight that you've seen?" I can think of several answers. The Grand Canyon. The Swiss Alps. Sequoia trees. The variety of animals on an African veldt.

But I sometimes answer, "My backyard."

If you could see my yard, you would say, "You've got to be kidding!" It's nothing special. Well, it is to me. Sitting on my porch, I can see the beauty of grass, flowers, and trees. I observe the variety of birds. Sometimes deer, foxes, and groundhogs visit. No, it is not as majestic a sight as the ones I mentioned, but those magnificent sights are often too much to take in. My backyard is astoundingly beautiful on a human scale. I can experience how its charms change from moment to moment and season to season.

It is the same way when I think of seeing God. The Almighty is too majestic to take in. I cannot imagine God, much less see Him. But God so much wanted us to see Him, that He became one of us. "So the Word became human and made his home among us. He was full of unfailing love and faithfulness. And we have seen his glory, the glory of the Father's one and only Son" (John 1:14).

GOD IN A BABY

The all-powerful God who is Spirit took on flesh. When the angel Gabriel appeared to Mary and told her she would have a child, she rightly asked, "But how can this happen? I am a virgin."

The angel replied, "The Holy Spirit will come upon you, and the power of the Most High will overshadow you. So the baby to be born will be holy, and he will be called the Son of God" (Luke 1:34-35).

God enters a womb. The God beyond all imagination is born just like we were born. He becomes a helpless baby. Many want to see that baby.

Ordinary, working-class people want to see Him. An angel appears to shepherds in a field and tells them the Messiah has been born in Bethlehem. An army of angels join in praise to God.

> When the angels had returned to heaven, the shepherds said to each other, "Let's go to Bethlehem! Let's see this thing that has happened, which the Lord has told us about."
>
> They hurried to the village and found Mary and Joseph. And there was the baby, lying in the manger. After seeing him, the shepherds told everyone what had happened and what the angel had said to them about this child. All who heard the shepherds' story were astonished.
>
> LUKE 2:15-18

Some think that shepherds in that time had a rough reputation (much like cowboys in the Old West). None of these shepherds were ever going to be a king, like David, but these common men see the face of God in a baby. They did not completely understand what they were seeing, but they knew God had acted and Messiah had come. They told others to come and see.

Prominent people also wanted to see this child.

> After this interview the wise men went their way. And the star they had seen in the east guided them to Bethlehem. It went ahead of them and stopped over the place where the child was. When they saw the star, they were filled with joy! They entered the house and saw the child with his mother, Mary, and they bowed down and worshiped him. Then they opened their treasure chests and gave him gifts of gold, frankincense, and myrrh.
>
> MATTHEW 2:9-11

Traditionally, we call these wise men the three kings. The Bible does not say they were kings or even that there were three of them, but they bring three kingly gifts to Jesus. They must have been wealthy enough to afford those gifts and to make the long journey to see this child. Perhaps they did not fully realize that they were seeing the face of God, but they knew enough to worship this king of the Jews.

Common people. Prominent people. One person had waited all his long life to see this child.

> At that time there was a man in Jerusalem named Simeon. He was righteous and devout and was eagerly waiting for the Messiah to come and rescue Israel. The Holy Spirit was upon

him and had revealed to him that he would not die until he
had seen the Lord's Messiah. That day the Spirit led him to
the Temple. So when Mary and Joseph came to present the
baby Jesus to the Lord as the law required, Simeon was there.
He took the child in his arms and praised God, saying,

> "Sovereign Lord, now let your servant die in peace,
> as you have promised.
> I have seen your salvation,
> which you have prepared for all people.
> He is a light to reveal God to the nations,
> and he is the glory of your people Israel!"
>
> LUKE 2:25-32

Salvation. Light to all the nations. Simeon sees the glory of God in the face of this child, the unseen God who lives in unapproachable light.

THE HUMAN FACE OF GOD

In the life of Jesus, we see what our God is like. "Christ is the visible image of the invisible God" (Colossians 1:15). We see God in the way Jesus treats the poor and helpless. We see the power of God in One who can still storms and multiply food. We see the compassion of God in the stories of healing. We see the redeeming God who came to seek and save the lost.

To give one example, consider the raising of Lazarus. There, we see a God touched by human suffering. "Jesus wept" (John 11:35). We see a God who is a friend to humanity. "The people who were standing nearby said, 'See how much he loved him!'" (John 11:36). We see a God who is angry at sin and at death, the result of sin (John 11:38). We see the glory of God. "Jesus responded, 'Didn't I tell you that you would see God's glory if you believe?'" (John 11:40). We witness a preview of what God will later do for Jesus and for us. Lazarus comes forth alive from the grave.

The apostles and others who witnessed this and other wonders should have known that Jesus was God, one with the Father. They still did not understand what they had seen. Like Moses, like Jacob, like us, they wanted to see the Father. One asks to do so.

> Philip said, "Lord, show us the Father, and we will be satisfied."
>
> Jesus replied, "Have I been with you all this time, Philip, and yet you still don't know who I am? Anyone who has seen me has seen the Father! So why are you asking me to show him to you? Don't you believe that I am in the Father and the Father is in me?
>
> JOHN 14:8-10

They do not see Jesus as who He truly is until after the resurrection. These disciples do not expect to see Jesus after His death. They think their hope in Him is in vain. He must not have been the One for whom they had waited, but then they see the resurrected Jesus. Mary Magdalene thinks the body of Jesus has been stolen. She asks the gardener near the empty tomb where the body might be. Then she hears Him say her name, "Mary." She then recognizes the risen Jesus (John 20:11-18). She tells the disciples, but they do not believe until they see Him with their own eyes. Later, many see the risen Jesus, even 500 of them at one time (1 Corinthians 15:6).

WE SEE BY FAITH

One is not there when the disciples see the risen Lord. He will not believe until he can see with his own eyes.

> One of the twelve disciples, Thomas (nicknamed the Twin), was not with the others when Jesus came. They told him, "We have seen the Lord!"
>
> But he replied, "I won't believe it unless I see the nail wounds in his hands, put my fingers into them, and place my hand into the wound in his side."
>
> Eight days later the disciples were together again, and this time Thomas was with them. The doors were locked; but suddenly, as before, Jesus was standing among them. "Peace be with you," he said. Then he said to Thomas, "Put your finger here, and look at my hands. Put your hand into the wound in my side. Don't be faithless any longer. Believe!"
>
> "My Lord and my God!" Thomas exclaimed.
>
> Then Jesus told him, "You believe because you have seen me. Blessed are those who believe without seeing me."
>
> JOHN 20:24-29

What would it have been like to see Jesus in the flesh? To look in His face and see the face of God? There were some who had that honor. One of them later writes, "We proclaim to you the one who existed from the beginning, whom we have heard and seen. We saw him with our own eyes and touched him with our own hands. He is the Word of life" (1 John 1:1).

But we have not seen Jesus.

Or have we?

Jesus says we are more blessed than those who saw Him with their own eyes. He blesses us because we believe without seeing. Yet we have seen Jesus. We see Him by faith. "To have faith is to be sure of the things we hope for, to be certain of the things we cannot see" (Hebrews 11:1, Good News Translation). "For our life is a matter of faith, not of sight" (2 Corinthians 5:7).

Faith is a new way of seeing. Through the eyes of faith, we see the baby in the manger, the one who raised Lazarus, and the one raised from the dead. We see the face of God in Jesus. That's why we must keep our focus on Him.

> Therefore, since we are surrounded by such a huge crowd of witnesses to the life of faith, let us strip off every weight that slows us down, especially the sin that so easily trips us up. And let us run with endurance the race God has set before us. We do this by keeping our eyes on Jesus, the champion who initiates and perfects our faith. Because of the joy awaiting him, he endured the cross, disregarding its shame. Now he is seated in the place of honor beside God's throne.
>
> HEBREWS 12:1-2

We keep our eyes on Jesus. We look at Him with eyes of love. "You love him even though you have never seen him. Though you do not see him now, you trust him; and you rejoice with a glorious, inexpressible joy. The reward for trusting him will be the salvation of your souls" (1 Peter 1:8-9).

WE WILL SEE HIS RETURN

The full salvation of our souls will happen when Jesus returns. If alive then, we will see Him with our eyes.

> Look! He comes with the clouds of heaven.
>   And everyone will see him—
>   even those who pierced him.
> And all the nations of the world
>   will mourn for him.
> Yes! Amen!
>
> REVELATION 1:7

If we die before Jesus comes, we have assurance that we will go and be with Him. We will see Him after death. What's more, we will see Him with the eyes of a resurrected body when He comes again. When that great day comes, we not only will see God in the face of Jesus, we will be like Him. "Dear friends, we are already God's children, but he has not yet shown us what we will be like when Christ appears. But we do know that we will be like him, for we will see him as he really is" (1 John 3:2).

Those who saw Him in the flesh did not see Him as He really was. Even those who believed in Him still asked to see the Father. But we know what He looks like. He looks like our loving Father. And the day will come when we see the face of God — Father, Son, and Spirit.

QUESTIONS FOR REFLECTION

1. Why did God become a human being?

2. Why did God choose shepherds to be the first to see Jesus?

3. What are the ways people saw God in Jesus during His ministry?

4. Why did Philip ask to see the Father? Why did he and the other disciples fail to see who Jesus was?

5. Wouldn't it have been better to be an eyewitness of Jesus than to have to see Him by faith? Why or why not?

6. How do we keep our focus on Jesus?

THREE
TASTING GOD

Genesis 2:7-9, Exodus 24:9-11, Deuteronomy 8:2-3, Isaiah 25:6, 55:1-2

As a fan of science fiction, I've always been fascinated by imaginings of the future. I still look forward to the day of flying cars, robots, teleportation, and easy space travel. What I never liked in those stories were the predictions of future meals. Nutritious and filling pills would take the place of the variety of food we have now.

"No thanks," I say. Give me food with taste, even if it might not be completely good for me. How could we live without the variety of tastes — sweet, sour, bitter, salty, and savory? What would be ideal is for our food to combine the best of tastes with filling us with everything we need to live healthy lives.

GOD GIVES TASTY FOOD

The God who shaped human bodies from the dust and breathed life into them also gave us hunger. He created us to eat. God gives us food, not bland and tasteless food, but what tastes good.

> Then the LORD God formed the man from the dust of the ground. He breathed the breath of life into the man's nostrils, and the man became a living person.
>
> Then the LORD God planted a garden in Eden in the east, and there he placed the man he had made. The LORD God made all sorts of trees grow up from the ground — trees that were beautiful and that produced delicious fruit.
>
> GENESIS 2:7-9

Why did God create us so that we would need food to live? Perhaps it was so that we would be dependent on Him for food (Psalm 145:15) and dependent on the land. Hunger reminds us that we are made by God and also made from dirt. God could have given us food pills with little taste. Instead, He gives us an amazing variety of attractive and delicious goodies. He gave humans the ability to prepare and serve those foods in creative ways. Even when the Lord gave Israel manna in the wilderness, it "tasted like honey" (Exodus 16:31).

The Lord not only gives the best of food, His care for us is like a feast, not an ordinary meal. The Lord is the best host and chef, "setting your table with the best food" (Job 36:16). He prepares a feast for us in the presence of our enemies (Psalm 23:5). He gives us daily bread (Matthew 6:11).

EATING WITH GOD

Sometimes God even invites His people to eat with Him. When Moses climbs Mount Sinai, the Lord at first does not let others come near. Later, God throws a party for Moses and the leaders of Israel.

> Then Moses, Aaron, Nadab, Abihu, and the seventy elders of Israel climbed up the mountain. There they saw the God of

> Israel. Under his feet there seemed to be a surface of brilliant blue lapis lazuli, as clear as the sky itself. And though these nobles of Israel gazed upon God, he did not destroy them. In fact, they ate a covenant meal, eating and drinking in his presence!
>
> EXODUS 24:9-11

This is startling in light of what we studied earlier. No one can see God, but here God eats with the leaders of His people. What do you suppose was on the menu? Would they even have noticed the food while eating in the glorious presence of the Lord?

Eating with the Lord was to be a regular occurrence in Israel through the sacrificial system. The peace offerings were meals, including meat, that the worshippers ate together as friends and family. What was left over on the third day of this feasting was to be burned up as an offering to God (Leviticus 7:11-18). God shared the food He provides with His people, and they, by their sacrifices, shared their food with God. This meal created and symbolized peace among people and peace between the Lord and His people. "There you and your families will feast in the presence of the LORD your God, and you will rejoice in all you have accomplished because the LORD your God has blessed you" (Deuteronomy 12:7).

Eating with God is such a rich experience that it is a *banquet* or *feast*. I have trouble relating to those words. *Banquet* sounds like one would have to wear uncomfortable clothes and eat a set, catered meal. *Feast* sounds like something out of the Middle Ages. Think instead of a Thanksgiving meal with all your favorite dishes eaten with the family you love. Imagine, too, a reunion dinner with old friends you have not seen for a while. That's the picture of eating with God.

The Lord invites us to this meal in the present. What's great is that it is free!

> "Is anyone thirsty?
>   Come and drink—
>   even if you have no money!
> Come, take your choice of wine or milk—
>   it's all free!
> Why spend your money on food that does not give you strength?
>   Why pay for food that does you no good?
> Listen to me, and you will eat what is good
>   You will enjoy the finest food."
>
> ISAIAH 55:1-2

I was always taught that there is no such thing as a free lunch. But there is! God still provides free food for His people.

This great meal with God is also in the future.

> In Jerusalem, the LORD of Heaven's Armies
>   will spread a wonderful feast
>   for all the people of the world.
> It will be a delicious banquet
>   with clear, well-aged wine and choice meat.
>
> ISAIAH 25:6

These and other Bible verse are not speaking of a literal, physical meal with God. Instead, the idea of sharing dinner with the Lord is a way of speaking of our entire life with God. This is why Jesus often spoke of the kingdom of God as a feast or banquet (Matthew 8:11-12, Luke 14:15-24). It will be like a king who throws a great wedding reception at the marriage of his son (Matthew 22:1-14).

God invites us to celebrate a meal with Him. He invites us not because we are worthy, but because He is a generous God. What we must do is to respond to His invitation and accept His free food. We do that by obeying Him and loving our neighbors.

HUNGRY FOR GOD

God gives us delicious food to eat. He invites us to His banquet table to enjoy life with Him. What's more, we are invited to feed on the delectable words of God. Psalm 119, the longest Psalm, tells repeatedly of the goodness of God's Word. "How sweet your words taste to me; they are sweeter than honey (Psalm 119:103). The prophet Ezekiel is fed a scroll of God's words; He says, "And when I ate it, it tasted as sweet as honey in my mouth" (Ezekiel 3:3).

Does God's Word taste sweet to you? Bible study can become a chore. If we think of the law of God as a set of picky rules that we must follow, then it's impossible to enjoy a word from God. Conversely, if we envisage the law as instruction of a loving Father to his dear children, then we can savor that word as a taste of honey. Meditating on the Word of God then becomes a delicious meal that we look forward to sharing. You don't have to call us to the table twice. We are eager to feast on the sweet words of the Lord.

God even compares the manna He gave to Israel to feed them physically with the words he gives them to nourish them spiritually.

> Remember how the Lord your God led you through the wilderness for these forty years, humbling you and testing you to prove your character, and to find out whether or not you would obey his commands. Yes, he humbled you by

letting you go hungry and then feeding you with manna, a food previously unknown to you and your ancestors. He did it to teach you that people do not live by bread alone; rather, we live by every word that comes from the mouth of the LORD.

DEUTERONOMY 8:2-3

If God is a loving Father, why would He want His beloved children to go hungry? It's for same reason every good parent has to teach their children how to eat. If you let kids choose their own menu, they always go for the junk food. We must encourage them to eat nutritious food. In time, they may even enjoy it. In the same way, God loves His people so much that He teaches them to feed on His Word — the Word that gives them life. They have "tasted the goodness of the word of God" (Hebrews 6:5).

God made us to be hungry. God wants us to be hungry. That's why the practice of fasting is so important in the Bible.

Examples of personal fasting of believers in the Bible:

1. King David fasted for the life of his infant son (2 Samuel 11:1-27, 2 Samuel 12:1-25).
2. When the word of the Lord concerning destruction came by Elijah to King Ahab of Israel for his grave sins, he fasted and mourned (1 Kings 21:17-29).
3. Ezra mourned, fasted, and prayed when he learned that not even the Levite priests had separated themselves from ungodly people and kept God's commandments (Ezra chapters 9 and 10).
4. King Darius the Mede fasted the night he threw Daniel into the lion's den (Daniel 6:1-28).

5. Daniel fasted and prayed for the forgiveness of the sins of Israel and their return to Jerusalem (Daniel 9:1-23).
6. The widow and prophetess Anna, fasted and prayed daily, in her service and worship of the Lord (Luke 2:36-38).
7. Jesus fasted 40 days and 40 nights while Satan tried to tempt him (Matthew 4:1-11, Mark 1:12-13, Luke 4:1-13).

Examples of corporate fasting of believers in the Bible:

1. The nation of Israel fasted on the Day of Atonement seeking forgiveness of sins (Exodus 30:10, Leviticus 16:2-34, Leviticus 23:26-32, Jeremiah 36:6, Acts 27:9, Hebrews 9:7, Hebrews 9:24-26).
2. The nation of Judah had four annual fast days (Zechariah 8:18-23), in which they would mourn the capture of Jerusalem in the fourth month of the year (Jeremiah 52:6-7), mourn the burning to the Lord's temple in the fifth month (2 Kings 25:8-11), mourn the murder of Gedaliah in the seventh month (Jeremiah 41:4), and mourn the attack on Jerusalem in the tenth month (Jeremiah 39:9-18, Jeremiah chapters 40-41).
3. The 11 tribes of Israel, who fought in a civil war against the tribe of Benjamin, wept and fasted before the Lord (Judges chapters 19-21).
4. King Jehoshaphat called Judah to a national fast to seek help from the Lord, when the Moabites, Ammonites, and Meunites came against them in war (2 Chronicles 20:1-30).

5. Daniel, Hananiah, Mishael, and Azariah fasted for three years on a diet of vegetables and water, so they would not defile themselves by the king of Babylon's food and wine (Daniel 1:5-21).
6. The nation of Nineveh fasted and repented when Jonah brought the message of destruction from the Lord because of their great wickedness (Jonah 3:1-10).
7. The disciples of John the Baptist fasted (Mark 2:18).
8. The 4,000 men who listened to Jesus, fasted for three days (Mark 8:1-9).
9. When Jesus returned to heaven, the apostles begin fasting (Matthew 9:15, Luke 5:34-35).
10. The early church at Antioch ministered before the Lord in fasting and prayer (Acts 13:1-3).
11. Paul and Barnabas fasted and prayed when appointing elders for each church the Lord had used them to start (Acts 14:23).

Why does God want us to fast? He does not want to make us miserable but to bring us joy. Fasting turns our hearts to God in gratitude and praise. That's what repentance is all about. God wants us empty, so He can fill us.

We feed on God's Word. We feed on God Himself. And He tastes good! The psalmist says, "Taste and see that the LORD is good" (Psalm 34:8). This is an invitation to experience God. You get to know someone by spending time with them, eating meals with them. We do lunch. We get coffee. In Bible study, prayer, meditation, and spending time with other Christians, we are getting to know the Lord. We eat with Him. We taste His goodness. "Like newborn babies, you must crave pure spiritual milk so that you will grow into a full experience of salvation. Cry out for this nourishment, now that you have had a taste of the Lord's kindness" (1 Peter 2:2-3).

SATISFIED BY GOD

I've only experienced haute cuisine once. That's a pretentious name for fancy food prepared by a famous chef. I was a guest of someone else who paid for the meal. I looked forward to the experience. However, when my plate came, I could not believe how tiny the portions were. Yes, it tasted good, but there was hardly enough to taste. *Oh, that's just the first course*, I thought. But no. That was the whole meal. When I got home, I had to find something else to eat.

We enjoy food that tastes wonderful, but we enjoy it more if there is enough of it. God not only tastes good, but He fills and satisfies us. "You satisfy me more than the richest feast.

I will praise you with songs of joy" (Psalm 63:5).

Nothing fully satisfies us in this life. We eat and soon are hungry again. We try to fill our lives with meaning through accomplishment, money, pleasure, alcohol, drugs, fame, beauty, health, comfort, and myriad other ways. None of them fill the hole in our soul.

This is why the Lord forbids idolatry. The gods of any age do not deliver what they promise. They cannot fill us. They cannot satisfy our desires; they only deepen them and frustrate us.

God made us to be hungry. He made us to be hungry for Him.

The Lord completely satisfies. He gives us tasty food to eat. He feeds us with His life-giving Word. He freely gives Himself to us and asks us to taste, eat, and be filled. "God blesses you who are hungry now, for you will be satisfied" (Luke 6:21).

Come to the table.

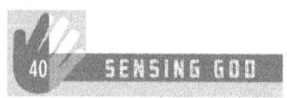

QUESTIONS FOR REFLECTION

1. Why do you think God created us to be hungry?

2. Why did God make taste?

3. How did Israel eat with God?

4. How do we eat with God today?

5. What are ways we can feed on the Word of God?

6. Have you tasted God? Does God taste good to you? Why?

FOUR
TASTING JESUS

John 2:9-10, John 6:35, 47-58, 1 Corinthians 10:16-18, Revelation 19:6-9

"I'm a vampire. I feed off the energy of my students."

So said a fellow college teacher many years ago. At first, the vampire language threw me, but I knew what he meant. The vibrant optimism of my young students also affected me. I fed off their interest and questions.

I've also had students who "fed off each other" in a negative way. When they were in class together, they tried to outdo one another in disrupting the learning of others. This is what the Bible warns about, "bad company corrupts good character" (1 Corinthians 15:33).

On the other hand, good companions shape our character. I am a better person because of the company I keep. For over 20 years, I have met weekly in a prayer group with four other men. Being with them each week gives me the focus and courage I need to continue as a disciple. I feed off their faith in struggles, their devotion to their wives and children, and their commitment to service to others.

Jesus invites us to feed off Him in a more intimate and dynamic way. We not only feed off His example of sacrificial love, but we taste the goodness of God in His life, death, and resurrection.

JESUS TASTED THE WORD OF GOD

As a human, Jesus knew what it was like to be hungry. At one point, He was extremely hungry. He had fasted for 40 days. He saw the nearby rocks that looked like small loaves of bread. Satan basically told Him, "Turn those rocks to tasty rolls." But Jesus would not. He had learned the lesson that God had taught Israel in the wilderness, "People do not live by bread alone, but by every word that comes from the mouth of God" (Matthew 4:4).

Why would it have been a sin for Jesus to turn those stones to bread? He was the Son of God. He had the power. He would later use that power to feed others, but He would not use it to feed Himself when He needed to be hungry for God. Jesus knew what tasted good. He knew what really satisfied. He had a craving for the word of God, even greater than His appetite for bread.

JESUS ATE WITH THE WRONG PEOPLE

Jesus knew hunger. That's why He's always eating in the gospel stories. People often invited Jesus to dinner, but they were the wrong kind of people.

> As Jesus was walking along, he saw a man named Matthew sitting at his tax collector's booth. "Follow me and be my disciple," Jesus said to him. So Matthew got up and followed him.

> Later, Matthew invited Jesus and his disciples to his home as dinner guests, along with many tax collectors and other disreputable sinners. But when the Pharisees saw this, they asked his disciples, "Why does your teacher eat with such scum?"
>
> When Jesus heard this, he said, "Healthy people don't need a doctor — sick people do."
>
> MATTHEW 9:9-12

We have lunch with friends, co-workers, and family, not with strangers. Jesus is part of the tax-collector, bad-sinner crowd. No wonder the respectable Pharisees objected. The reply of Jesus about doctors says much about the Pharisees. There are two types of sinners — those who know they are sick and go to the doctor and those who will not admit their illness. The Pharisees were in great danger because they had the deadly disease of sin but would not come to Doctor Jesus for the cure.

Interestingly, Jesus also accepted dinner invitations from Pharisees. An immoral woman interrupted one such dinner by anointing the feet of Jesus, washing His feet with her tears, and even kissing His feet. This display greatly offended Simon the Pharisee, the host of the meal. Jesus responded by telling the story of two men who owed money: one owed 500 pieces of silver, the other owed 50. The lender forgave both of their debts. Jesus then asks Simon, "Who do you suppose loved him more after that?" He replies, "The one forgiven the most" (see Luke 7:36-50). The point was not that the woman was a worse sinner than Simon. The point was that, unlike Simon, she *knew* she was a forgiven sinner.

Another time a Pharisee had Jesus to dinner, then criticized Him for not washing correctly, that is, the Pharisee way. Jesus takes the opportunity to rebuke the Pharisees for concern for the outward appearance of cleanliness while neglecting true purity of heart (Luke 11:37-54). Jesus eats with a leader of the Pharisees and reprimands the diners for taking the best seats at the table. He says, "For those who exalt themselves will be humbled, and those who humble themselves will be exalted" (Luke 14:1-24).

Jesus knew how to be hungry. He wanted to taste the goodness of God. When He ate, He wanted His dinner companions to be hungry for God, so He ate with the worst sinners, even the Pharisees.

JESUS FED OTHERS

Like God the Father, Jesus provided food to others. Like God, He gave the tastiest food and gave enough to fill them.

The first miracle or sign that Jesus did was turning water to wine at a wedding feast. It was a huge amount of wine, 120 to 180 gallons. And it was the best quality.

> When the master of ceremonies tasted the water that was now wine, not knowing where it had come from (though, of course, the servants knew), he called the bridegroom over. "A host always serves the best wine first," he said. "Then, when everyone has had a lot to drink, he brings out the less expensive wine. But you have kept the best until now!"
>
> JOHN 2:9-10

The only miracle found in all four Gospels (except for the Resurrection) is the feeding of the 5,000 (Matthew 14:13–21; Mark 6:31–44; Luke 9:12–17; John 6:1–14). Matthew and Mark also tell of the feeding of the 4,000 (Matthew 15:32–39, Mark 8:1–9). In both cases, Jesus multiplies a few loaves and fish to fill the stomachs of everyone in the crowd and still have some left over. As God made tasty food for humans in Eden and fed Israel with manna in the wilderness, so Jesus provides for those who hear Him.

FEEDING ON JESUS
These miraculous meals give Jesus a chance to tell of the most delicious and nutritious food.

> Jesus replied, "I am the bread of life. Whoever comes to me will never be hungry again. Whoever believes in me will never be thirsty."
>
> "I tell you the truth, anyone who believes has eternal life. Yes, I am the bread of life! Your ancestors ate manna in the wilderness, but they all died. Anyone who eats the bread from heaven, however, will never die. I am the living bread that came down from heaven. Anyone who eats this bread will live forever; and this bread, which I will offer so the world may live, is my flesh."
>
> Then the people began arguing with each other about what he meant. "How can this man give us his flesh to eat?" they asked.
>
> So Jesus said again, "I tell you the truth, unless you eat the flesh of the Son of Man and drink his blood, you cannot have eternal life within you. But anyone who eats my flesh and drinks my blood has eternal life, and I will raise that person at the last day. For my flesh is true food, and my blood is true drink. Anyone who eats my flesh and drinks my blood remains in me, and I in him. I live because of the living Father who sent me; in the same way, anyone who feeds on me will live because of me. I am the true bread that came down from heaven. Anyone who eats this bread will not die

as your ancestors did (even though they ate the manna) but will live forever."

JOHN 6:35, 47-58

Jesus is speaking to those who had eaten the loaves and fish He provided. They are willing to accept free food from Jesus but not willing to eat His flesh and drink His blood. Clearly, Jesus was not promoting cannibalism, but He was calling them to be His disciples and feed on Him.

Are we different from this crowd? We want Jesus to bless us, and He does. He gives us food to eat. He gives us all we need. "We are so blessed," we say, and we are. Jesus, however, wants much more from us. He wants us to be so close to Him that we consume Him. We depend on Him alone. He wants every part of our body and every part of our lives to be dependent on the nourishment that He alone provides. Without manna, Israel would have starved. Without Jesus, so do we.

THE LORD'S SUPPER

When we think of eating the body of Jesus and drinking His blood, we think of the Lord's Supper. On the night He was betrayed, Jesus took bread, blessed it, and said, "Take this and eat it, for this is my body." And he took a cup of wine and gave thanks to God for it. He gave it to them and said, "Each of you drink from it, for this is my blood, which confirms the covenant between God and his people. It is poured out as a sacrifice to forgive the sins of many" (Matthew 26:26-28).

Jesus said, "Do this in remembrance of me" (Luke 22:19). He could have told his disciples to think of Him now and then. Instead, He gave them bread and wine that they could taste.

He gave them as part of a larger meal, the Passover, that was a memorial of God's delivering Israel from slavery.

What we eat at the Lord's Supper is not much of a meal, a bit of bread and a sip of juice. It does not fill our stomachs or quench our thirst. Yet the Supper is the most delectable and nutritious food we can eat. We are eating the body and drinking the blood of Jesus.

Someone once challenged me on that.

"Do you mean the body and blood of Jesus are physically present in the Lord's Supper?" "No," I replied. "But it is spiritually present."

"Oh, spiritually present," he said. "I thought you meant Jesus was really present."

We should never contrast the spiritual with the real. The spiritual is more permanent, more real, than the physical. In the Supper, through our sense of taste, we reenter the death and resurrection of Jesus. We participate in those events. Jesus described His suffering as drinking a bitter cup (Matthew 20:22, 26:39). On the cross, He "tasted death for everyone" (Hebrews 2:9). That's why Paul says,

> When we bless the cup at the Lord's Table, aren't we sharing in the blood of Christ? And when we break the bread, aren't we sharing in the body of Christ? And though we are many, we all eat from one loaf of bread, showing that we are one body. Think about the people of Israel. Weren't they united by eating the sacrifices at the altar?
>
> 1 CORINTHIANS 10:16-18

Just as Israel ate with the Lord God in the peace offerings, so we eat with Jesus at the Supper. More than that, we taste His body and blood.

If we believe Christ is present in the bread and wine, our prayers will change and our hearts will change in communion. The Lord's Supper will take on the same importance as baptism. Something happens here! In baptism, we are born anew spiritually through the blood of Christ. We are joined with our brothers and sisters in Christ. After birth, we need food. In the supper, we spiritually eat and drink the body and blood of Christ. By this meal, our souls are fed. If we believe this, then the Supper will become more than just a command to obey, more than an example to follow, more than just a symbol. It becomes food and drink to us, nourishing our faith, filling us with the presence of Christ. Is this not the heart of worship, to praise our God for what God has done for us in Christ and to enjoy Him forever?

EATING WITH THE RESURRECTED JESUS

After His resurrection, Jesus continued to eat with His disciples (Luke 24:41-43, John 21:9-12). When Cleopas and his friend were on the way to Emmaus, the risen Jesus joined them on the road, but they did not recognize Him until He broke bread with them (Luke 24:30-35). Why did Jesus eat after His resurrection? Perhaps He wanted to assure the disciples that He was no ghost. Maybe even a resurrected body gets hungry. Most of all, He still wanted to have the deep friendship with His followers that only comes through tasting food together.

We also will eat with the resurrected Jesus. Jesus promises, "Look! I stand at the door and knock. If you hear my voice and open the door, I will come in, and we will share a meal together as friends" (Revelation 3:20). This great meal in the age to come is a wedding feast — and we are the bride!

> Then I heard again what sounded like the shout of a vast crowd or the roar of mighty ocean waves or the crash of loud thunder:
> "Praise the Lord!
> For the Lord our God, the Almighty, reigns.
> Let us be glad and rejoice,
> and let us give honor to him.
> For the time has come for the wedding feast of the Lamb,
> and his bride has prepared herself.
> She has been given the finest of pure white linen to wear."
> For the fine linen represents the good deeds of God's holy people.
> And the angel said to me, "Write this: Blessed are those who are invited to the wedding feast of the Lamb."
>
> REVELATION 19:6-9

Jesus invites us to taste Him now. He invites us to taste Him in eternity at the great wedding feast where the church is joined to the victorious Lamb. Taste! Eat!

QUESTIONS FOR REFLECTION

1. What does it mean to live by the Word of God, not by bread alone?

2. Why is it good news that Jesus ate with sinners?

3. Should we eat with sinners? Why or why not?

4. How does Jesus provide food for us?

5. What are some ways that we eat the body of Jesus?

6. What is the mood at a wedding reception? What does that say about the heavenly wedding feast we will enjoy?

FIVE

SMELLING GOD

Genesis 8:20-21, Psalm 45:6-8, 115:4-6, Isaiah 1:13, 65:1-5, Romans 12:1, 2 Corinthians 2:14-16, Hebrews 13:15-16

Of all the senses, smell has the worst reputation. If I say, "That smells," you don't think I mean it has a pleasing aroma. I mean it stinks. There's something slightly embarrassing and humorous about smell. "You smell funny" is not a compliment. We also smell with our noses, and they also can be comic, depending on their size and shape.

Smell is the underrated sense. It is much more important than we realize. That is clear when we lose our sense of smell. I have a friend who lost his ability to smell anything. That affects his appetite, his mood, and even his safety. After all, there are smells that warn us of danger.

There are an immense variety of smells. If you walk to work each morning taking the same route, the sights are almost always the same. The smells, though, may differ from day to day and block to block. Smell connects us to our environment and to other people. It has considerable influence on sexual attraction, which is why there is a multi-billion dollar industry of perfumes and other fragrances. Smell can also bring back memories from the distant past.

God gave us smell. Like all our senses, He gave it, so we could enjoy His gifts and use our sense of smell to glorify Him.

GOD CAN SMELL

When we say that God can smell, we are speaking of Him in human terms. God is Spirit (John 4:24). He is beyond our imagination, but we must describe Him in some way. Since humans are the greatest creations of the Lord, the Bible often speaks of God in human terms.

The Lord predicts that Israel will abandon Him: "There, in a foreign land, you will worship idols made from wood and stone — gods that neither see nor hear nor eat nor smell" (Deuteronomy 4:28). Those gods do not exist. That's why they cannot smell.

The psalmist makes the same argument about idols shaped in human form:

> Their idols are merely things of silver and gold,
>   shaped by human hands.
> They have mouths but cannot speak,
>   and eyes but cannot see.
> They have ears but cannot hear,
>   and noses but cannot smell.
>
> PSALM 115:4-6

The implication is that the Living God can smell. He knows what our lives are like. He smells our fears, our joys, our desperation, and our trust.

GOD SMELLS SACRIFICES

Why is it important that God can smell? It's because He smells the smoke of the sacrifices that His people made. Leaving the ark after the flood, Noah makes one of the earliest burnt offerings in the Bible.

> Then Noah built an altar to the LORD, and there he sacrificed as burnt offerings the animals and birds that had been approved for that purpose. And the LORD was pleased with the aroma of the sacrifice and said to himself, "I will never again curse the ground because of the human race, even though everything they think or imagine is bent toward evil from childhood. I will never again destroy all living things."
>
> GENESIS 8:20-21

The ancient world thought that the gods depended on sacrifices as their meals. If humans did not sacrifice, the gods would starve. There is none of that idea here. The Lord is in control over all living things. He does not need sacrifices for sustenance. The Lord enjoys the sweet smell of Noah's sacrifice because it expresses Noah's gratitude for his salvation from the flood. In response to what he smells, God promises never again to destroy all living things.

The burnt offerings of the Israelites are also "a pleasing aroma, a special gift presented to the Lord" (Exodus 29:18, 25, 41). It is a beautiful portrait of the relationship between God and His people. Their sacrifices are not empty rituals but express their desire to please God. They want to smell good to Him.

Israel also burned incense to the Lord that literally smelled good. The Bible speaks of prayers as incense. The psalmist prays, "Accept my prayer as incense offered to you, and my upraised hands as an evening offering" (Psalm 141:2). In Revelation, 24 elders praise the slaughtered Lamb, "Each one had a harp, and they held gold bowls filled with incense, which are the prayers of God's people" (Revelation 5:8). Later ". . . another angel with a gold incense burner came and stood at the altar. And a great amount of incense was given to him to mix with the prayers of God's people as an offering on the gold altar before the throne" (Revelation 8:3).

How wonderful to think that our prayers are not a bother to God but a lovely perfume! God wants to hear His children. He even wants to smell them. Do you remember the smell of your children? The same affection that a parent has for their newborn is how God feels about us.

And we, like Israel, make sacrifices to God.

> And so, dear brothers and sisters, I plead with you to give your bodies to God because of all he has done for you. Let them be a living and holy sacrifice — the kind he will find acceptable. This is truly the way to worship him.
>
> ROMANS 12:1

> Therefore, let us offer through Jesus a continual sacrifice of praise to God, proclaiming our allegiance to his name. And don't forget to do good and to share with those in need. These are the sacrifices that please God.
>
> HEBREWS 13:15-16

These verses say that our sacrifices are pleasing and acceptable to God. We give our whole bodies to Him in praise and in service. Even if they do not mention God smelling our sacrifices, I believe He does. We smell good to the God who loves us, who gives us life, and who asks that we give our lives back to Him.

GOD SMELLS US

God's people smell good to Him. Good smells, however, can turn bad. Israel abandons exclusive worship to the Lord and goes after idols. They begin to stink before the Lord.

> The LORD says,
> "I was ready to respond, but no one asked for help.
>   I was ready to be found, but no one was looking for me.
> I said, 'Here I am, here I am!'
>   to a nation that did not call on my name.
> All day long I opened my arms to a rebellious people.
>   But they follow their own evil paths
>   and their own crooked schemes.
> All day long they insult me to my face
>   by worshiping idols in their sacred gardens.
>   They burn incense on pagan altars.
> At night they go out among the graves,
>   worshiping the dead.
> They eat the flesh of pigs
>   and make stews with other forbidden foods.
> Yet they say to each other,
>   'Don't come too close or you will defile me!
>   I am holier than you!'
> These people are a stench in my nostrils,
>   an acrid smell that never goes away."
>
> ISAIAH 65:1-5

We've all had those terrible smells that won't go away. God's people once smelled like perfume, but now they stink (Isaiah 3:24). They keep offering their sacrifices to the Lord while at the same time they worship the gods of their time. God would rather have them stop worshiping Him altogether! Even their incense has a disgusting smell.

> Stop bringing me your meaningless gifts;
> the incense of your offerings disgusts me!
> As for your celebrations of the new moon and the Sabbath
> and your special days for fasting—
> they are all sinful and false.
> I want no more of your pious meetings.
>
> ISAIAH 1:13

We cannot bring our sacrifices of praise and service to God and at the same time follow the ways of our culture. We dare not praise God on Sunday and live like the rest of the world on other days. God demands our entire devotion. He wants all of us. If we try to serve the Lord and serve ourselves or other "gods," we become a nauseating odor that God cannot get out of His nostrils.

Even though God speaks that way about Israel, there is hope of restoration if they turn to Him: "When I bring you home from exile, you will be like a pleasing sacrifice to me. And I will display my holiness through you as all the nations watch" (Ezekiel 20:41). If we also turn from the idolatry of our time, God will bring us out of exile. Again, our sacrifices will smell good to Him.

SMELLING LIKE CHRIST

Our sacrifices smell good to God. They may not smell good to others. Paul talks of his ministry in terms of smell.

> But thank God! He has made us his captives and continues to lead us along in Christ's triumphal procession. Now he uses us to spread the knowledge of Christ everywhere, like a sweet

> perfume. Our lives are a Christ-like fragrance rising up to God. But this fragrance is perceived differently by those who are being saved and by those who are perishing. To those who are perishing, we are a dreadful smell of death and doom. But to those who are being saved, we are a life-giving perfume. And who is adequate for such a task as this?
>
> 2 CORINTHIANS 2:14-16

Like Paul, all Christians should smell like Jesus. And how did Jesus smell? We'll talk about that more in the next chapter, but smelling like Jesus means having the sacrificial love that Jesus has. Paul had shown that love to the Corinthians through his sufferings on their behalf. When we sacrificially serve others in the name of Jesus, a marvelous fragrance rises up to God. Those who are being saved can smell it, too.

We don't, however, smell nice to everyone. We bring the world good news! Jesus has died for the sins of the world. God wants everyone to be saved, but there will always be some who only smell death and doom on us. They will falsely accuse us of hating them. They will call us narrow and judgmental hypocrites. When Jesus brought the good news, they crucified Him. We should not think it strange that what smells good to God may smell awful to others. We have to choose whose nose we wish to please.

DOES GOD SMELL GOOD TO US?

The Bible speaks often of God smelling us. Only one passage speaks of how God smells.

> Your throne, O God, endures forever and ever.
>> You rule with a scepter of justice.
>
> You love justice and hate evil.

> Therefore God, your God, has anointed you,
>> pouring out the oil of joy on you more than on anyone else.
> Myrrh, aloes, and cassia perfume your robes.
>> In ivory palaces the music of strings entertains you.
>
> PSALM 45:6-8

This psalm may refer to God or to the king or to the Anointed One or Messiah who is to come. That one has perfumed robes. His robes are fragrant. He smells delectable.

We want to smell good to God. We confess that He smells good to us. Like the joy that comes from smelling a flower or the best perfume or new-mown grass, we rejoice in the Lord.

QUESTIONS FOR DISCUSSION

1. Why do we sometimes neglect or even make fun of our sense of smell?

2. Why does the Bible describe God in human terms?

3. What comes to mind when you think of sacrifices?

4. How are our prayers like incense to God?

5. When do we smell bad to God?

6. How can we smell sweet to others spiritually?

SMELLING JESUS

Luke 7:36-48, John 19:38-42, Ephesians 5:1-2

Several years ago, I was the guest preacher at a small downtown church. I entered and sat on the second row. Soon a man came, greeted me, and sat in front of me. From his clothes, I thought he might have been homeless. It wasn't his clothes I noticed; it was his smell. He stank. So much so that I found myself breathing through my mouth and even holding my breath. I smelled him during the singing. I smelled him when I got up to preach. After the worship, the church had a meal together. Guess who sat beside me?

Yet I greeted him as a brother and treated him with kindness. Why? Because I'm such a good Christian that I can stoop to his level? No. Such an attitude would be nothing but patronizing pride. Why did I greet him as a brother in spite of his smell? For the same reason he greeted me as a brother. We shared a common humanity. To be human is to smell. For all I know, this brother thought I smelled bad, too. For all I know, I did. God has blessed us with the inability to smell ourselves.

JESUS SMELLED

Have you ever thought how Jesus must have smelled. Was there a whiff of holiness around Him? Did He have a heavenly cologne that drew others to Him?

Perhaps the Jesus of our imagination smelled that way, but not the flesh-and-blood Jesus. He lived in a culture that did not bathe as often as we do. He lived before the invention of deodorants, although (as we shall see) they did have perfumes and ointments to help their scent. He worked as a carpenter or builder. No offense to those in the construction industry, but after they have a grueling day at work, you might not want to stand too close to them. So it likely was with Jesus. Even in His ministry, He walked miles on dusty roads and had no permanent home. He may have smelled like my homeless friend.

If all this talk of smell and stink puts you off, especially about our Lord Jesus, let me remind you that the heart of the good news is that "the Word became flesh" (John 1:14, NIV). As you know, flesh does not always smell nice. That's why in most of the stories of Jesus that involve smell, someone is enhancing His aroma.

THE SMELL OF A BABY

The first gifts that Jesus receives are gold, frankincense, and myrrh from the wise men (Matthew 2:11). Frankincense was an ingredient in the incense burned in the tabernacle and the temple (Exodus 30:34-38). It was to be sprinkled on the grain offerings of the Israelites, "a pleasing aroma to the LORD" (Leviticus 2:1-2). Myrrh was part of the mixture of spices Moses used to anoint the vessels of the tabernacle and to anoint Aaron and his sons as priests (Exodus 30:22-33).

In addition to their biblical significance, some today use frankincense and myrrh in healing. They fight bacteria, heal wounds, and function as essential oils. They have a spicy, fragrant scent.

Many have speculated on what Joseph and Mary did with the gifts from the wise men. Some think they sold them to pay for their lodging in Bethlehem and even for their stay in Egypt. Others say they sold the gold for those purposes but used the frankincense to freshen the stable or home where they lived. Mary then used the myrrh as baby oil for Jesus.

Babies smell. When the smell is bad, we give them back to their parents to change. Conversely, then there is that marvelous clean baby smell, enhanced by baby lotion. Jesus was a baby like all babies. Perhaps He smelled like frankincense and myrrh.

SMELLY FEET

There are three stories of women anointing the feet of Jesus.

> One of the Pharisees asked Jesus to have dinner with him, so Jesus went to his home and sat down to eat. When a certain immoral woman from that city heard he was eating there, she brought a beautiful alabaster jar filled with expensive perfume. Then she knelt behind him at his feet, weeping. Her tears fell on his feet, and she wiped them off with her hair. Then she kept kissing his feet and putting perfume on them.
>
> When the Pharisee who had invited him saw this, he said to himself, "If this man were a prophet, he would know what kind of woman is touching him. She's a sinner!"

Then Jesus answered his thoughts. "Simon," he said to the Pharisee, "I have something to say to you."

"Go ahead, Teacher," Simon replied.

Then Jesus told him this story: "A man loaned money to two people — 500 pieces of silver to one and 50 pieces to the other. But neither of them could repay him, so he kindly forgave them both, canceling their debts. Who do you suppose loved him more after that?"

Simon answered, "I suppose the one for whom he canceled the larger debt."

"That's right," Jesus said. Then he turned to the woman and said to Simon, "Look at this woman kneeling here. When I entered your home, you didn't offer me water to wash the dust from my feet, but she has washed them with her tears and wiped them with her hair. You didn't greet me with a kiss, but from the time I first came in, she has not stopped kissing my feet. You neglected the courtesy of olive oil to anoint my head, but she has anointed my feet with rare perfume.

"I tell you, her sins — and they are many — have been forgiven, so she has shown me much love. But a person who is forgiven little shows only little love." Then Jesus said to the woman, "Your sins are forgiven."

LUKE 7:36-48

Simon, the respectable Pharisee, is shocked. This immoral woman (and we know what kind of woman she is) invades his house. She then brazenly anoints, washes, dries (with her hair), and kisses the feet of Jesus. What an affront to propriety!

It is Simon, though, who has done what is improper. He has failed to wash the feet of Jesus before the meal. Why is that significant? In that time, most people ate in a reclining position, which meant someone's feet would be near your face. Eating next to someone who had walked all day on a dusty road would be a smelly experience if someone had not washed their feet. Simon should have done this out of basic hospitality. As a Pharisee, he should have done it because he knew it was biblical (Genesis 18:4, 19:2, 24:32, 43:24, Exodus 30:18-21, Judges 19:21, 1 Samuel 25:41).

Why did Simon not wash Jesus' feet or at least have a servant do it? Maybe he was trying to humiliate Jesus. He invites Him to dinner with other "respectable" people who would ridicule this upstart Rabbi with His smelly feet. Whatever the reason, Jesus turns the woman's act of love into a lesson on forgiveness and gratitude.

In the second episode of anointing feet, Mary of Bethany anoints the feet of Jesus with costly perfume to express her deep gratitude for the raising of her brother, Lazarus. She also wipes the feet of Jesus with her hair. Here, Jesus eats with dear friends, not someone trying to get the best of him. No doubt they had already washed the feet of Jesus, but Mary wanted to do more. His feet were clean and did not smell bad. Mary wanted him to enjoy the scent and feel of this expensive perfume. Jesus said she did it in preparation for his burial, which was only a week later (John 12:1-3).

Just two days before Passover and His betrayal and arrest, Jesus went to the house of another Simon, a healed leper in Bethany. This time, a woman anoints not His feet but His head. Some object to the cost of the perfume, but Jesus tells them to leave her alone for she has anointed Him for burial. He adds, "I tell you the truth, wherever the Good News is preached throughout the world, this woman's deed will be remembered and discussed" (Mark 14:1-9, Matthew 26:6-13).

Unlike feet, the head of Jesus likely did not have a bad scent. Now, it has a delightful odor. One wonders if that smell lingered with Jesus through His trial and crucifixion. If so, if must have brought Him some comfort.

What's the significance of anointing? *Messiah* or *Christ* means "anointed one." Aaron and his sons became priests of God by being anointed with oil (Exodus 28:41). Samuel anoints Saul (1 Samuel 10:1) and later David (1 Samuel 16:23) to be king. Elijah anoints Elisha to make him a prophet (1 Kings 19:16). Anointing marks Jesus as the ultimate priest, king, and prophet. He is God's Messiah.

Washing and anointing feet were also an act of hospitality. Later, Jesus will wash the disciples' feet. Here women wash and anoint His feet, providing the welcome that the hosts neglected to provide.

Let us not forget the smell. The sense of smell awakens memories more than the other senses. When Jesus smelled this perfume, He thought of the love and gratitude of those women. Jesus might have smelled bad to others. He was a fragrant Savior to them.

THE SMELL OF DEATH

Jesus hears that his friend, Lazarus, is sick. He delays visiting him, and Lazarus dies. Then Jesus visits. Arriving at their home in Bethany, Jesus meets the sisters of Lazarus: Martha and Mary, each of whom says, "Lord, if only you had been here, my brother would not have died" (John 11:21 and 32). The sisters believed in the power of Jesus to heal. What they did not expect is for Jesus to raise Lazarus from the dead.

That is clear when they make a visit to the tomb, and Jesus asks them to roll the stone away from the entrance. "But Martha, the dead man's sister, protested, 'Lord, he has been dead for four days. The smell will be terrible'" (John 11:39).

Dead bodies stink. Their smell reminds us of what God said to Adam after the first sin, "For you were made from dust, and to dust you will return" (Genesis 3:19).

But Jesus does not avoid the stench of dead. He calls Lazarus forth from the tomb. He proves he is "the resurrection and the life" (John 11:25). Jesus changes the stink of death into the fragrance of new life.

Jesus Himself will reek of death. After His death on the cross, two secret disciples of Jesus work to prevent the smell of death.

> Afterward Joseph of Arimathea, who had been a secret disciple of Jesus (because he feared the Jewish leaders), asked Pilate for permission to take down Jesus' body. When Pilate gave permission, Joseph came and took the body away. With him came Nicodemus, the man who had come to Jesus at night. He brought about seventy-five pounds of perfumed ointment made from myrrh and aloes. Following Jewish burial custom, they wrapped Jesus' body with the spices in long sheets of linen cloth. The place of crucifixion was near a garden, where there was a new tomb, never used before. And so, because it was the day of preparation for the Jewish Passover and since the tomb was close at hand, they laid Jesus there.
>
> JOHN 19:38-42

Seventy-five pounds of perfumed ointment! It took a tremendous amount of fragrance to overcome the stink of decomposition. Some women in the life of Jesus must not have known that Joseph and Nicodemus had done this because they also brought burial spices to anoint the body on the Sunday after His death (Mark 16:1). Or perhaps they wanted to add their gift to that of the two men. Either way, the women do not get to anoint the body of Jesus because it had been raised from the dead. The One who is the resurrection and the life had obliterated the stench of death once and for all, not only for His own body, but for the bodies of all who trust Him.

JESUS SMELLS GOOD

The sacrifice of Jesus on the cross, even more than all the sacrifices under the Law, smells good to God.

> Imitate God, therefore, in everything you do, because you are his dear children. Live a life filled with love, following the example of Christ. He loved us and offered himself as a sacrifice for us, a pleasing aroma to God.
>
> EPHESIANS 5:1-2

We are to imitate God who gave His Son as a sweet-smelling sacrifice for our sins. "Our lives are a Christ-like fragrance rising up to God" (2 Corinthians 2:15). We smell like Christ when we serve others in His name through acts great and small. When the Philippians send a gift to Paul to support his ministry, he reacts by saying, "I am generously supplied with the gifts you sent me with Epaphroditus. They are a sweet-smelling sacrifice that is acceptable and pleasing to God" (Philippians 4:18).

So, as followers of the flesh-and-blood Jesus who smelled bad to some but was a sweet fragrance to God, let us perfume each day with acts of selfless service in the name of Jesus.

QUESTIONS FOR REFLECTION

1. What do people smell like? What do you smell like? What did Jesus smell like?

2. What do you think about your feet? The feet of others? The feet of Jesus?

3. What were the reasons the three women anointed Jesus?

4. Why is the stench of death more than simply an unpleasant smell?

5. How can we smell like Jesus?

TOUCHING GOD

Exodus 19:11-12, 2 Samuel 6:3-7, Isaiah 6:1-8, 41:10-13, Hosea 11:3-4

Touch is the most intimate of the senses. I don't usually mind when people look at me, listen to me, speak to me, or even smell me (as long as they don't get too close). I'm more selective about who I want to touch me. Touching requires a relationship built on experience and trust.

We even use the word *touch* to enhance our language about the other senses. "Her words touched my heart." "When I saw how he treated his mother, it was touching." "The scented candles at the party were a nice touch."

DON'T TOUCH GOD

Since touch is the most intimate sense, we might be surprised that the Lord commands His people *not* to touch Him.

> Be sure they are ready on the third day, for on that day the LORD will come down on Mount Sinai as all the people watch.

> Mark off a boundary all around the mountain. Warn the people, "Be careful! Do not go up on the mountain or even touch its boundaries. Anyone who touches the mountain will certainly be put to death."
>
> EXODUS 19:11-12

The holy Presence of the Lord descends on Mount Sinai. God's people are to keep their distance.

Why? Does God not love His people? Does God want to be distant from them? Yes, He loves them. That's why He delivered them from Egyptian slavery. That's why He comes near to them on the mountain. But the Lord is not a "safe" God. You cannot manipulate Him. He is God, and we are not.

Years ago, every week we passed an electrical substation near our church. There was a large sign on it, "Danger! High Voltage!" If you walked near it, your hair would stand on end from the electrical current. I was glad for that substation because it supplied power to our neighborhood, but I did not get too close. It's the same with the Lord.

Later, God warns His people not to touch even the sacred objects in the tabernacle, or they would die (Numbers 4:15). Later in their history, a man named Uzzah ignores that warning with fatal consequences.

> They placed the Ark of God on a new cart and brought it from Abinadab's house, which was on a hill. Uzzah and Ahio, Abinadab's sons, were guiding the cart that carried the Ark of God. Ahio walked in front of the Ark. David and all the people of Israel were celebrating before the LORD, singing songs and playing all kinds of musical instruments — lyres, harps, tambourines, castanets, and cymbals.

> But when they arrived at the threshing floor of Nacon, the oxen stumbled, and Uzzah reached out his hand and steadied the Ark of God. Then the Lord's anger was aroused against Uzzah, and God struck him dead because of this. So Uzzah died right there beside the Ark of God.
>
> 2 SAMUEL 6:3-7

We might feel that Uzzah was only trying to keep the Ark of the Covenant safe, but the Lord's Holy Presence was in the Ark. Touching the Lord is not safe.

GOD TOUCHES US

Touching the Lord is forbidden. Even touching the mountain when He is there or touching the Ark is not safe. But the Lord often touches His people. He can initiate the touch. We may not.

The first time the Lord interacts with humanity, it is with a touch. "Then the Lord God formed the man from the dust of the ground. He breathed the breath of life into the man's nostrils, and the man became a living person" (Genesis 2:7). The picture here is of a potter forming us from clay (Isaiah 64:8). God creates humans by getting His hands dirty. He touches. He shapes us. He then breathes life into us. A loving touch begins our life with the Lord our God.

The Lord gave a special touch to certain persons to call them and empower them for His service. When Samuel anoints Saul to be king of Israel, it says, "When Saul returned to his home at Gibeah, a group of men whose hearts God had touched went with him" (1 Samuel 10:26). We don't know exactly how God touched their hearts, but Saul needed good men to walk alongside him. The Lord provided those helpers.

God touches Isaiah to make him a prophet.

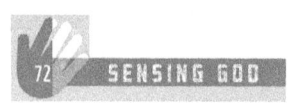

> It was in the year King Uzziah died that I saw the Lord. He was sitting on a lofty throne, and the train of his robe filled the Temple. Attending him were mighty seraphim, each having six wings. With two wings they covered their faces, with two they covered their feet, and with two they flew. They were calling out to each other,
>
> > "Holy, holy, holy is the LORD of Heaven's Armies!
> > The whole earth is filled with his glory!"
>
> Their voices shook the Temple to its foundations, and the entire building was filled with smoke.
>
> Then I said, "It's all over! I am doomed, for I am a sinful man. I have filthy lips, and I live among a people with filthy lips. Yet I have seen the King, the LORD of Heaven's Armies."
>
> Then one of the seraphim flew to me with a burning coal he had taken from the altar with a pair of tongs. He touched my lips with it and said, "See, this coal has touched your lips. Now your guilt is removed, and your sins are forgiven."
>
> Then I heard the Lord asking, "Whom should I send as a messenger to this people? Who will go for us?"
>
> I said, "Here I am. Send me."
>
> ISAIAH 6:1-8

Seeing the Lord is not enough for Isaiah. Seeing God only shows how sinful Isaiah and his people are. It takes the touch of God to remove Isaiah's guilt and to make him ready to answer God's call.

God touches other prophets. Jeremiah is to speak for God. "Then the LORD reached out and touched my mouth and said, 'Look, I have put my words in your mouth!'" (Jeremiah 1:9). The Lord grabs Ezekiel. "The LORD gave this message to Ezekiel son of Buzi, a priest, beside the Kebar River in the land of the

Babylonians, and he felt the hand of the Lord take hold of him" (Ezekiel 1:3). God's hand lifts up Daniel. "Just then a hand touched me and lifted me, still trembling, to my hands and knees" (Daniel 10:10).

True prophets are never self-made. It takes the powerful, yet gentle hand of God to cleanse them, take hold of them, and put the word in their mouths.

The touch of God is glorious, but it is also demanding. It is not easy to be a prophet. The touch of God cost them their families, their safety, and sometimes their lives. Remember when the Lord wrestled with Jacob? He touched Jacob. The result was a pain in the hip (Genesis 32:25). We want the touch of God, but it is, at times, a painful touch.

GOD HOLDS US

The touch of the Lord can be painful, but most of the time it is a healing and protecting touch. When trouble comes and there seems to be no relief, the loving hand of God is there to hold us.

> Don't be afraid, for I am with you.
>> Don't be discouraged, for I am your God.
> I will strengthen you and help you.
>> I will hold you up with my victorious right hand.
>> "See, all your angry enemies lie there,
>> confused and humiliated.
> Anyone who opposes you will die
>> and come to nothing.
>> You will look in vain
>> for those who tried to conquer you.
> Those who attack you
>> will come to nothing.

> For I hold you by your right hand—
> I, the LORD your God.
> And I say to you,
> 'Don't be afraid. I am here to help you."
>
> ISAIAH 41:10-13

Like the psalmist, we cry, "Reach down from heaven and rescue me; rescue me from deep waters, from the power of my enemies" (Psalm 144:7). And God hears our cry! How marvelous in times of trouble to feel God stretch out his hand to hold ours. His powerful right hand pours strength into our weak hand.

God's touch is as gentle as the hands of a nurse with a hurting patient. "He heals the brokenhearted and bandages their wounds" (Psalm 147:3). The worst agony is an aching heart. No power on earth can completely heal a broken heart. The One who formed us from the dust reaches down again to repair our hearts with His tender hands.

The touch of God is like a mother's touch.

> It was I who taught Ephraim to walk,
>   taking them by the arms;
> but they did not realize
>   it was I who healed them.
> I led them with cords of human kindness,
>   with ties of love.
> To them I was like one who lifts
>   a little child to the cheek,
>   and I bent down to feed them.
>
> HOSEA 11:3-4 (NIV)

The Almighty God who warns His people not to touch Him stoops down and holds His children in His arms. When they take their first steps, He is there to make sure they do not fall. He holds us to His cheeks. Like a mother, He cradles us in His arms and feeds us. Can there be a greater portrait of our closeness to God?

A friend once brought his newborn pug puppy for me to see. I could hold it in my hand. It was weak and small but adorable. I remember showing it to everyone around me. That's what we are to God. He holds us in His hand. He thinks the world of us. "The Lord will hold you in his hand for all to see — a splendid crown in the hand of God" (Isaiah 62:3).

The touch of God changes us forever. That touch calls us, forgives us, empowers us, protects us, feeds us, heals us, and proudly displays us for all to see.

QUESTIONS FOR REFLECTION

1. When do you want to be touched? When do you not want anyone to touch you?

2. Why would God warn His people not to touch Him?

3. Why did God kill Uzzah for touching the Ark of the Covenant?

4. Why does the Lord touch people to make them prophets?

5. What are the blessings God gives through touch?

6. How is God like a mother?

EIGHT
TOUCHING JESUS

Matthew 17:5-8, 19:13-15, Mark 5:24-34, 40-42, Luke 7:14-15, John 20:26-29, 1 John 1:1

Have you met Taylor Swift?

If you don't know who that is, just substitute the name of someone famous you'd like to meet.

Before you answer the Taylor Swift question, let's think about what we mean by "met." You could answer, "I went to one of her concerts." That only means that you saw her from a distance along with thousands of other people. That isn't really meeting her. Or you could say, "I saw her once walking through a store." But surrounded by her bodyguards and so far way, you barely recognized her.

However, if you say, "I shook her hand, chatted with her, and even (with permission) put my hand around her shoulders and took a selfie," then you met Taylor Swift.

Have you met God? You've heard about Him, seen Him from a distance (in a sense), and talked to Him in prayer. But have you shaken His hand or felt His arms around your shoulder? What if you could touch God with your own hands? Some did.

> We proclaim to you the one who existed from the beginning, whom we have heard and seen. We saw him with our own eyes and touched him with our own hands. He is the Word of life.
>
> 1 JOHN 1:1

THE HEALING TOUCH

God touches us to bind our wounds and heal our broken hearts (Psalm 147:3). As God-in-the-flesh, Jesus does the same, healing with His touch.

Here are some Jesus touched to heal:

- A person with leprosy in Galilee (Matthew 8:2-3, Mark 1:40-42, Luke 5:12-13).
- Peter's mother in law in Capernaum (Matthew 8:14-15, Mark 1:30-31).
- Several people in a crowd in Capernaum (Luke 4:40).
- Two blind men in Capernaum (Matthew 9:29-30).
- A few people in Nazareth (Mark 6:4-6).
- A deaf man (Mark 7:32-35).
- A blind man just outside Bethsaida (Mark 8:22-25).
- A blind man in Jerusalem (John 9:1, 6-7).
- A bent woman in the synagogue (Luke 13:11-13).
- Two blind men near Jericho (Matthew 20:30-34).

One story focuses on a woman who touched Jesus, not on Jesus having touched her.

Jesus went with him, and all the people followed, crowding around him. A woman in the crowd had suffered for twelve years with constant bleeding. She had suffered a great deal from many doctors, and over the years she had spent everything she had to pay them, but she had gotten no better. In fact, she had gotten worse. She had heard about Jesus, so she came up behind him through the crowd and touched his robe. For she thought to herself, "If I can just touch his robe, I will be healed." Immediately the bleeding stopped, and she could feel in her body that she had been healed of her terrible condition.

Jesus realized at once that healing power had gone out from him, so he turned around in the crowd and asked, "Who touched my robe?"

His disciples said to him, "Look at this crowd pressing around you. How can you ask, 'Who touched me?'"

But he kept on looking around to see who had done it. Then the frightened woman, trembling at the realization of what had happened to her, came and fell to her knees in front of him and told him what she had done. And he said to her, "Daughter, your faith has made you well. Go in peace. Your suffering is over."

MARK 5:24-34

This story is between the two halves of the story of Jairus, who asks Jesus to heal his little daughter who is near death. The urgent journey to heal the girl is interrupted by this woman. She desperately wants the touch of Jesus, but she wants to do it secretly. We aren't sure why. Was she ceremonial unclean and afraid to make Jesus unclean? Was she nervous as a woman to touch a great rabbi? Did she want to avoid detaining Jesus on

His mission of mercy for Jairus? Was she just shy? Whatever her reluctance, she trusts the power of Jesus to heal. She touches the edge of His robe, and that power binds her wounds.

Jesus is sensitive to those around Him. He knows the difference between the jostle of the crowd and the touch of faith. When the woman reveals her touch, Jesus touches her heart with words of gentle encouragement. Others like her would touch the edge of the robe of Jesus and find healing (Mark 6:56, Matthew 14:36).

One odd story of the touch of Jesus is how he heals a man who was born blind. "Then he spit on the ground, made mud with the saliva, and spread the mud over the blind man's eyes. He told him, "Go wash yourself in the pool of Siloam" (Siloam means "sent"). So the man went and washed and came back seeing!" (John 9:6-7). Many speculate on why Jesus made mud instead of simply touching the man's eyes. Might this be an echo of the touch of God in creating humans from the dust of the ground (Genesis 2:7)? Jesus is creating the eyes of this man anew, a preview of the new creation to come. Jesus has the creative touch of God.

THE TOUCH OF BLESSING

The disciples sometimes do not want people to bother Jesus for His touch.

> One day some parents brought their children to Jesus so he could lay his hands on them and pray for them. But the disciples scolded the parents for bothering him.
>
> But Jesus said, "Let the children come to me. Don't stop them! For the Kingdom of Heaven belongs to those who are

like these children." And he placed his hands on their heads and blessed them before he left.

MATTHEW 19:13-15

Why did the disciples scold these parents? Did they think children would disrupt the ministry of Jesus? Were children too unimportant for the busy Jesus? We've all had children who interfere with our busy schedules. At times, the kids even interrupt church! To Jesus, the children who seek Him are an example to us all. We all need the touch of blessing from His hands.

Some of these same disciples, three in the inner circle of Jesus, had earlier felt His uplifting touch. Peter, James, and John see Jesus transfigured on the mountain, alongside Moses and Elijah. Peter suggests building shrines for all three — placing Jesus on the same level as the great lawgiver and the great prophet.

> But even as he spoke, a bright cloud overshadowed them, and a voice from the cloud said, "This is my dearly loved Son, who brings me great joy. Listen to him." The disciples were terrified and fell face down on the ground.
>
> Then Jesus came over and touched them. "Get up," he said. "Don't be afraid." And when they looked up, Moses and Elijah were gone, and they saw only Jesus.
>
> MATTHEW 17:5-8

At different times, Moses and Elijah had heard the voice of God on Mount Sinai with smoke and fire and lightning and earthquakes (Exodus 19:16-20, 1 Kings 19:11-13). They responded with fear. Here on another mountain these three disciples see the glory of God and hear His voice in Jesus alone. The sight and sound terrify them, but the gentle touch of Jesus takes away their fear.

We also have felt the assuring touch of Jesus. He has taken away our fear. So we must not, like these disciples, stop others we consider to be weak and inconsequential from coming to receive a blessing from His hands.

THE TOUCH OF RESURRECTION

Jesus heals and blesses with His touch. He also has life in His caress. When He raises Lazarus, He does it with His voice. Conversely, when Jesus raises children from the dead, He does it with the tender touch of His hand.

The healing of the bleeding woman delays the visit of Jesus to heal the young daughter of Jairus. By the time they get to the house where she was, she is dead. Those there say, "Do not bother the Teacher. There's nothing he can do now." But He can. Jesus says the girl is not dead but asleep. Those who believe her to be dead laugh at Him.

> After he put them all out, he took the child's father and mother and the disciples who were with him, and went in where the child was. He took her by the hand and said to her, "Talitha koum!" (which means "Little girl, I say to you, get up!"). Immediately the girl stood up and began to walk around (she was twelve years old). At this they were completely astonished.
>
> MARK 5:40-42, NIV

Just as God led Israel by His life-giving hand, so Jesus gives life with a touch.

On another occasion, Jesus meets a funeral procession coming from the village of Nain. The dead young man is the only son of his mother. Jesus interrupts the funeral with a touch.

> Then he went up and touched the bier they were carrying him on, and the bearers stood still. He said, "Young man, I say to you, get up!" The dead man sat up and began to talk, and Jesus gave him back to his mother.
>
> LUKE 7:14-15

A 12-year old girl and a young man who was the only support of his widowed mother. Jesus could have raised them from the dead in many ways. He chooses to touch the dead bodies, making Him unclean in the eyes of the Law (Numbers 19:11). Jesus knows that it is death itself that is the ultimate uncleanness. His caress makes them clean with the gift of life.

TOUCHING THE RESURRECTED ONE

There are two stories of someone touching the resurrected body of Jesus. In one, Jesus says not to touch Him. In the other, He commands that touch. In each case, He says what He does to assure those who touch Him of the reality of His resurrection.

Mary Magdalene comes to the empty tomb and thinks someone has taken the body of Jesus. She sees someone who she believes is a gardener. When He says her name, she recognizes the resurrected Jesus and joyfully embraces Him. "Don't cling to me," Jesus said, "for I haven't yet ascended to the Father. But go find my brothers and tell them, 'I am ascending to my Father and your Father, to my God and your God'" (John 20:17).

It could be that Jesus is telling her not to touch Him at all, but likely He is trying to get her to let go of Him, so she can tell others of the resurrection. Mary has found her Lord and does not want to stop hugging Him. When Jesus says He has not yet ascended, He is reassuring her that He is not a ghost. She and the other disciples will have more chances to be with Him before He ascends.

Mary tells the disciples, "I have seen the Lord" (John 20:18). As she is talking, Jesus Himself appears in the room, showing them the wounds in His hands and side, so they will believe.

But Thomas is not with them. He refuses to believe until he sees the wounds and touches them himself.

> Eight days later the disciples were together again, and this time Thomas was with them. The doors were locked; but suddenly, as before, Jesus was standing among them. "Peace be with you," he said. Then he said to Thomas, "Put your finger here, and look at my hands. Put your hand into the wound in my side. Don't be faithless any longer. Believe!"
> "My Lord and my God!" Thomas exclaimed.
> Then Jesus told him, "You believe because you have seen me. Blessed are those who believe without seeing me."
>
> JOHN 20:26-29

When Thomas touches Jesus, he breaks out with the most profound confession of the Gospels, "My Lord and my God" (John 20:28). The one Thomas has touched is the God of Israel. He is the One who formed humans from the dust. He is the One who has the hands of healing and the touch of life.

THE CONTINUING TOUCH

Let's return to the verse at the beginning of this chapter.

> We proclaim to you the one who existed from the beginning, whom we have heard and seen. We saw him with our own eyes and touched him with our own hands. He is the Word of life.
>
> 1 JOHN 1:1

John, Thomas, and many others touched Jesus with their own hands. When they touched Him, they did not fully realize who they had their hands on. Only after the ascension and the coming of the Spirit at Pentecost did they begin to comprehend that they were touching God, the One who existed in the beginning.

We have not touched Jesus with our hands, yet we felt His blessing as children. His hands bound our wounds when we were desperate for relief. His caress has soothed our fears. The day will come when He touches our mortal bodies and gives them everlasting life. He touched me. He touched you. We have met Jesus.

QUESTIONS FOR REFLECTION

1. In what sense have we met Jesus?

2. Why does Jesus heal so many with a touch instead of just a word?

3. Is there anyone who should not receive the touch of Jesus? Why forbid children to come to Him?

4. Why is touch so important when one is raised from the dead?

5. Can we cling too much to Jesus? Must we let Him go to do what He asks of us?

6. How has Jesus touched you?

NINE
HEARING GOD

Genesis 2:15-17, Exodus 3:4-10, Deuteronomy 6:1-9, 1 Samuel 3:1-10, Isaiah 30:19-21

I live in Nashville, so I hear my fair share of country music. I hear it in stores, restaurants, and elevators. I can hear live country music at many venues near me.

I must confess; I don't generally like country music. My biggest problem with it is that I don't understand the words. What I mean is, I can't clearly hear the words. There may be two reasons for this. Country singers generally do not articulate clearly. A Southern drawl is part of the nature of the music. They just don't speak plainly! That's the explanation I prefer.

The other possibility is that my hearing is going bad. That's the explanation I do not like nor want to admit.

When it comes to hearing God, we can blame Him for our lack of understanding. If only the Lord would make things plain. Many have made that excuse. The truth is that God has spoken.

We may not understand all that He has said, but we understand enough. The problem is not in God's articulation but in our hearing.

What a tragedy that would be to have to make our way in the world led only by what we hear from others! Words bombard us each day. Billboards, websites, podcasts, radio, television, not to mention the people around us, all have advice and "truth" for us. How can we decide who to hear?

Good news! The Lord has not left us on our own to do our best without His guidance. God has spoken and continues to speak in many ways. His words are true and powerful.

WE HEAR GOD IN CREATION

The word of God is so powerful that He spoke the world into existence. "Let there be," God said in the beginning. "Let there be light, (Genesis 1:3), space between the waters (Genesis 1:6), dry land (Genesis 1:9), plants (Genesis 1:11), sun and moon (Genesis 1:14-18), fish (Genesis 1:20), and animals (Genesis 1:24)" said the Lord. And it was so. The whole of creation hears the voice of God calling it into being.

But God made one thing that could refuse to hear. "Then God said, "Let us make human beings in our image, to be like us" (Genesis 1:26). God spoke directly to Adam.

> The LORD God placed the man in the Garden of Eden to tend and watch over it. But the LORD God warned him, "You may freely eat the fruit of every tree in the garden — except the tree of the knowledge of good and evil. If you eat its fruit, you are sure to die."
>
> GENESIS 2:15-17

Adam and Eve heard the Lord, but didn't listen to Him. They ate the fruit. Sin entered the world. The next time they heard God walking in the garden, they tried to hide from Him because they were naked and ashamed. God pronounced punishment on their sin, but even though they hadn't listened to God, He did not stop talking to them. His words of judgment were words of love, showing that the Lord had not abandoned them.

HEARING GOD'S CALL

The Lord spoke to Noah, telling of the coming flood and commanding Noah to build the ark to save his family and the animals. Noah heard. "So Noah did everything exactly as God had commanded him" (Genesis 6:22).

Abraham heard the call of God to leave his homeland and go to a new land where he would be a blessing to all the families of the earth. "So Abram departed as the Lord had instructed" (Genesis 12:4). From Abraham, Isaac, and Jacob, all of whom heard the voice of God, would come the people of Israel.

When Egypt enslaved the Israelites, they cried out to the Lord. The Lord responded by calling Moses from a burning bush.

> When the Lord saw Moses coming to take a closer look, God called to him from the middle of the bush, "Moses! Moses!"
>
> "Here I am!" Moses replied.
>
> "Do not come any closer," the Lord warned. "Take off your sandals, for you are standing on holy ground. I am the God of your father — the God of Abraham, the God of Isaac, and the God of Jacob." When Moses heard this, he covered his face because he was afraid to look at God.
>
> Then the Lord told him, "I have certainly seen the oppression of my people in Egypt. I have heard their cries of

> distress because of their harsh slave drivers. Yes, I am aware of their suffering. So I have come down to rescue them from the power of the Egyptians and lead them out of Egypt into their own fertile and spacious land. It is a land flowing with milk and honey — the land where the Canaanites, Hittites, Amorites, Perizzites, Hivites, and Jebusites now live. Look! The cry of the people of Israel has reached me, and I have seen how harshly the Egyptians abuse them. Now go, for I am sending you to Pharaoh. You must lead my people Israel out of Egypt."
>
> EXODUS 3:4-10

After making several attempts to avoid God's call, Moses finally went to Egypt. He took the word of the Lord to Pharaoh who would not hear it until the plague killed his firstborn son. Pharaoh let God's people go, changed his mind, and pursued them with his army. The Lord led Israel through the Red Sea on dry land but drowned Pharaoh and his army.

Then at Mount Sinai the Lord spoke to Moses, giving instruction to his people, all of whom heard him. "The LORD spoke these words to all of you assembled there at the foot of the mountain. He spoke with a loud voice from the heart of the fire, surrounded by clouds and deep darkness. This was all he said at that time, and he wrote his words on two stone tablets and gave them to me" (Deuteronomy 5:22).

Later, the Lord spoke to His people through judges, kings, and prophets. Over 400 times in the Old Testament we have this phrase, "This is what the Lord says." God continually spoke to His people, encouraging, warning, and instructing them out of love.

LISTENING TO GOD

Often, God's people will not listen to Him. They go their own way. They follow other gods. They have heard the voice of God, but they do not or cannot understand. The Lord has spoken clearly. That is not the problem. The problem is with their hearing.

Like a frustrated parent, the Lord gets tired of talking to children who will not listen. For a while, He will not talk to them. They do not hear the voice of God. At one point, His voice is so rare that it is not recognized when He does decide to speak.

> Meanwhile, the boy Samuel served the Lord by assisting Eli. Now in those days messages from the Lord were very rare, and visions were quite uncommon.
>
> One night Eli, who was almost blind by now, had gone to bed. The lamp of God had not yet gone out, and Samuel was sleeping in the Tabernacle near the Ark of God. Suddenly the Lord called out, "Samuel!"
>
> "Yes?" Samuel replied. "What is it?" He got up and ran to Eli. "Here I am. Did you call me?"
>
> "I didn't call you," Eli replied. "Go back to bed." So he did.
>
> Then the Lord called out again, "Samuel!"
>
> Again Samuel got up and went to Eli. "Here I am. Did you call me?"
>
> "I didn't call you, my son," Eli said. "Go back to bed."
>
> Samuel did not yet know the Lord because he had never had a message from the Lord before. So the Lord called a third time, and once more Samuel got up and went to Eli. "Here I am. Did you call me?"
>
> Then Eli realized it was the Lord who was calling the boy. So he said to Samuel, "Go and lie down again, and

if someone calls again, say, 'Speak, LORD, your servant is listening.'" So Samuel went back to bed.

And the LORD came and called as before, "Samuel! Samuel!"

And Samuel replied, "Speak, your servant is listening."

1 SAMUEL 3:1-10

You can ignore the voice of the Lord for so long that you cannot hear it. That is what happened to Eli. As God's priest, he should have been attuned to God's voice, but it took him three times before he realized it was the Lord who talked to Samuel.

There is a grave warning here to us as the people of God. The Lord speaks to us in many ways — through Scripture, events, and people. Are we listening, or has His voice become so unfamiliar to us that we can no longer hear?

In fairness to Eli, he does give the boy, Samuel, the only proper response to the voice of the Lord. "Speak, your servant is listening." The Lord may have to speak our names more than three times to get our attention. When we do hear, we must respond by listening.

The Israelites later refuse to hear God so often that He sent them into exile. Even then, He promised to speak to them and guide them if they would turn their hearts to Him.

> O people of Zion, who live in Jerusalem,
>   you will weep no more.
> He will be gracious if you ask for help.
>   He will surely respond to the sound of your cries.
> Though the Lord gave you adversity for food
>   and suffering for drink,
> he will still be with you to teach you.
>   You will see your teacher with your own eyes.

> Your own ears will hear him.
>> Right behind you a voice will say,
> "This is the way you should go,"
>> whether to the right or to the left.
>>> ISAIAH 30:19-21

God still longs to be gracious to His people. He hears our cries for help. He tells us which way to go. Our own ears hear Him.

TO HEAR IS TO OBEY

If we truly hear God, we will do what He says. In the Bible, to hear means to obey. This is clear in the most repeated verses of the Old Testament, heard every Sabbath in the synagogue.

> "These are the commands, decrees, and regulations that the LORD your God commanded me to teach you. You must obey them in the land you are about to enter and occupy, and you and your children and grandchildren must fear the LORD your God as long as you live. If you obey all his decrees and commands, you will enjoy a long life. Listen closely, Israel, and be careful to obey. Then all will go well with you, and you will have many children in the land flowing with milk and honey, just as the LORD, the God of your ancestors, promised you.
>
> "Listen, O Israel! The LORD is our God, the LORD alone. And you must love the LORD your God with all your heart, all your soul, and all your strength. And you must commit yourselves wholeheartedly to these commands that I am giving you today. Repeat them again and again to your children. Talk about them when you are at home and when you are on the road, when you are going to bed and when you are getting

up. Tie them to your hands and wear them on your forehead as reminders. Write them on the doorposts of your house and on your gates."

DEUTERONOMY 6:1-9

This great statement of faith is called the "Shema" after the Hebrew word that means "hear" or "listen." To hear God is to love Him with all our heart, soul, and strength. To hear is to obey. If we hear, we then tell those precious words to our children. We talk of them all the time. That's why Jesus quotes this passage and calls it the greatest command (Matthew 22:36-40).

God has spoken! What wonderful news! But if we do not obey what God has said, out of love for Him, we have not heard. If we do not pass His word to our children, we have not heard. If we know our Bibles backward and forward, but do not follow its teachings, we do not hear. "But don't just listen to God's word. You must do what it says. Otherwise, you are only fooling yourselves" (James 1:22).

Hear God. Listen. Do.

QUESTIONS FOR REFLECTION

1. How do we hear God in creation?

2. Does God always speak clearly?

3. How can we hear a word of judgment from God?

4. What are some ways you have heard the voice of God?

5. What does it take to hear the voice of God?

6. Do we always want to hear God? Why or why not?

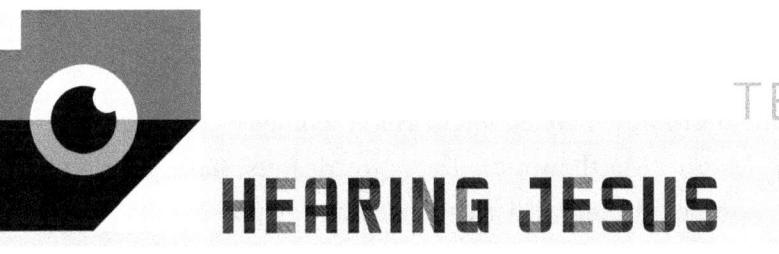

TEN
HEARING JESUS

Matthew 7:24-27, 13:10-13, John 4:39-42, 5:28-29, 10:24-27, 1 John 5:13-15

Imagine that you cannot read.

That's hard to do while you are reading this book.

For most of human history, the vast majority of people could not read or write. How did they learn? By sight, through observation. By touch, through apprenticeships. Most of all, they learned by hearing. Even today, many educational psychologists say we learn more from hearing than from seeing.

In the days of Jesus, well over 90 percent of the population could not read. They had to hear to learn. That's why Jesus taught orally and why He speaks often of hearing and listening. His words astonished His listeners. Even we who can read need to listen to what we read and what we hear from Jesus.

HEAR THE TEACHER
Imagine what it would have been like to hear Jesus teach with

your own ears. How fresh those words would be! Would we have understood them? Would His teaching have shocked us?

As it is, the teachings of Jesus might be too familiar to us. Take the best-known collection of His teachings — the Sermon on the Mount (Matthew 5-7). Those words must have puzzled those who heard them. It isn't the rich and happy people who are blessed by God. It's the poor, hungry, sad, and persecuted. You must be more righteous than the Pharisees! Outward obedience does no good if you commit adultery and murder people in your heart. Love your enemies! Pray for those who harm you. You cannot serve God and money. Don't worry about the basics of life, not even food and clothing. Do to others whatever you would like them to do to you.

These words from Jesus do not surprise us. They are quite familiar. In my experience, we try to explain them away. Turning the other cheek and loving our enemies do not work in the real world. We find creative ways to serve both God and money. Or so we think. We turn these commands of Jesus into hyperbole, exaggerated teachings that no one expects us to follow. Some turn the entire Sermon on the Mount into an impossible dream. Jesus is giving us a target to shoot at that is beyond our abilities. He is showing us what we cannot do to drive us to grace.

But Jesus expected His original listeners to hear and obey His words. That's why He ends the sermon like this:

> "Anyone who listens to my teaching and follows it is wise, like a person who builds a house on solid rock. Though the rain comes in torrents and the floodwaters rise and the winds beat against that house, it won't collapse because it is built on bedrock. But anyone who hears my teaching and doesn't obey it is foolish, like a person who builds a house on sand.

> When the rains and floods come and the winds beat against that house, it will collapse with a mighty crash."
>
> MATTHEW 7:24-27

We do not hear the teaching of Jesus unless we obey it. If we dismiss His instruction as irrelevant to daily life, we are fools. We are fooling ourselves by thinking we are followers of Jesus without obeying Him. We may call Him "Lord," but we do not recognize his authority over every moment of our lives. Those who heard Him with their own ears were struck by that authority. "When Jesus had finished saying these things, the crowds were amazed at his teaching, for he taught with real authority — quite unlike their teachers of religious law" (Matthew 7:28-29).

Jesus challenged those who heard Him. He sometimes intentionally spoke in riddles, so His hearers would seek the deeper meaning of His words. He called those riddles "parables."

> His disciples came and asked him, "Why do you use parables when you talk to the people?"
>
> He replied, "You are permitted to understand the secrets of the Kingdom of Heaven, but others are not. To those who listen to my teaching, more understanding will be given, and they will have an abundance of knowledge. But for those who are not listening, even what little understanding they have will be taken away from them. That is why I use these parables,
>
> For they look, but they don't really see.
> They hear, but they don't really listen or understand."
>
> MATTHEW 13:10-13

If we fall into the habit of listening to Jesus but not doing what He says, then we are not hearing Him. We may study His words each week but be deaf to them. Jesus taught in parables so that those who genuinely wanted to hear Him would ask, "What does this mean?" Then He would give them abundant knowledge.

The Bible experts of His day and ours were certain that they understood the Scriptures, but they did not obey them. They had ears but could not hear. In His teaching, Jesus often said, "Anyone with ears to hear should listen and understand" (Matthew 13:9). Their deafness was not of the ears but of the heart. "For the hearts of these people are hardened, and their ears cannot hear, and they have closed their eyes — so their eyes cannot see, and their ears cannot hear, and their hearts cannot understand, and they cannot turn to me and let me heal them" (Matthew 13:15). Jesus healed the deaf (Mark 7:31-37), but He could not heal those deaf of heart. He could not because they would not admit their loss of hearing.

Can we hear the teaching of Jesus? "Of course we can," you might say, "Right now, we are studying a book on the Bible."

Might it be that our own familiarity with the teaching of Jesus makes us deaf to His words? Are we like the Pharisees and experts in the Bible who think we hear but do not obey?

May God open the ears of our hearts to the life-giving words of Jesus.

HEARING AND FAITH

Jesus intended His words to create trust in Him. Those who hear come to believe that He is the Messiah, the promised one. Sometimes that faith came through the words of others who had heard Jesus. Sometimes, it is firsthand. Jesus has a conversation with a Samaritan women by a well. His knowledge of her leads her to believe He is the Messiah and to go to her village and spread the news. The villagers want to hear for themselves.

> Many Samaritans from the village believed in Jesus because the woman had said, "He told me everything I ever did!" When they came out to see him, they begged him to stay in their village. So he stayed for two days, long enough for many more to hear his message and believe. Then they said to the woman, "Now we believe, not just because of what you told us, but because we have heard him ourselves. Now we know that he is indeed the Savior of the world."
>
> JOHN 4:39-42

The Bible experts of the time would not listen to Jesus. Those experts thought the Samaritans were beyond the reach of the Messiah. But these hated Samaritans hear Jesus for themselves and confess their faith in the strongest language, "We know he is indeed the Savior of the world" (John 4:42). They are willing to listen.

Contrast that with those who have heard but will not believe. Jesus says He is the great Shepherd of His flock. Who belongs to that flock? Those who hear His voice, trust Him, and follow.

> The people surrounded him and asked, "How long are you going to keep us in suspense? If you are the Messiah, tell us plainly."
>
> Jesus replied, "I have already told you, and you don't believe me. The proof is the work I do in my Father's name. But you don't believe me because you are not my sheep. My sheep listen to my voice; I know them, and they follow me."
>
> JOHN 10:24-27

Something mysterious happens when people hear the Word of God through Jesus. That word is powerful enough to create saving trust in some who hear. "But not everyone welcomes the Good News, for Isaiah the prophet said, "LORD, who has believed our message?" So faith comes from hearing, that is, hearing the Good News about Christ" (Romans 10:16-17). Part of the mystery is that some will not hear the good news. How can anyone reject good news? The answer is that they do not trust that news. Perhaps they think it is too good to be true. Full and free salvation is hard to believe.

Do we trust the good news? Do we accept our acceptance by God because of Jesus? Do we genuinely believe that He is our shepherd? Do we listen for His voice?

HEARING AND RESURRECTION

Jesus often healed by speaking. Those who heard His words immediately received health. One heard Him and came from the grave. "Then Jesus shouted, 'Lazarus, come out!' And the dead man came out, his hands and feet bound in graveclothes, his face wrapped in a headcloth. Jesus told them, 'Unwrap him and let him go!'" (John 11:43-44). Hearing Jesus brought life to Lazarus.

He is not the only one who will hear the voice of Jesus and live again.

> Don't be so surprised! Indeed, the time is coming when all the dead in their graves will hear the voice of God's Son, and they will rise again. Those who have done good will rise to experience eternal life, and those who have continued in evil will rise to experience judgment.
>
> JOHN 5:28-29

When those who trust in Jesus die, they go to be with the Lord, but that is not their final destiny. They wait to hear the voice of Jesus, so their bodies will rise again. Then they will be forever with the Lord in a new heaven and earth.

How important is it to listen to Jesus? Our lives depend on it. That's true not only after we die, but even now, we must pay attention to His words of life. At one point, many deserted Jesus, causing Him to ask the 12 apostles, "Are you also going to leave?" Simon Peter replied, "Lord, to whom would we go? You have the words that give eternal life" (John 6:68). If we want to have life now and in eternity, we must listen to Jesus.

LISTENING FOR JESUS

We listen to the teaching of Jesus. His words create trust in Him. His words give us life.

Jesus promises more than mere words. He wants to come into our lives, to make His home with us. "Look! I stand at the door and knock. If you hear my voice and open the door, I will come in, and we will share a meal together as friends" (Revelation 3:20).

What does it take to hear Jesus knocking? It requires concentration. We must eliminate the noise that keeps us from hearing His knock. Noise surrounds us. We distract ourselves by media, busyness, and worry. We let the voices of those around us tell us who we are instead of listening for the one voice that matters. To hear Jesus, we must quiet our hearts.

It takes practice to hear Jesus. We must discipline ourselves to have a regular time for Bible study and for prayer. We practice service to others, especially when it is not convenient, so we may hear the voice of the One who came to serve.

We need help to hear Jesus. That's why church is so essential to discipleship. We need to hear Jesus speak to us through others who hear and obey Him. We need their wisdom to discern His voice.

Jesus is knocking. Will we answer?

JESUS HEARS US

We sometimes fail to listen to Jesus. We do not always pay attention to His call. We listen to other voices or our own voice, not His.

Jesus knows that and understands. We can be confident of our standing with Jesus not because of our great ability to hear Him, but because He always hears us.

> I have written this to you who believe in the name of the Son of God, so that you may know you have eternal life. And we are confident that he hears us whenever we ask for anything that pleases him. And since we know he hears us when we make our requests, we also know that he will give us what we ask for.
>
> 1 JOHN 5:13-15

The loving Jesus hears our prayers. He gives us what we ask for. How can that be? We have all made requests of Jesus and not received what we asked for. But Jesus taught us by His word and by His example how to pray the prayer that never fails — "Your will, not mine, be done." The greatest request we make of Jesus is that we will hear Him. We ask Him to enter us when we knock. We ask that His will be done. And He always answers!

May Jesus open the ears of our hearts to hear Him.

QUESTIONS FOR REFLECTION

1. Do you learn the most from what you hear?

2. What are some ways we try to explain away the teaching of Jesus?

3. How did hearing bring you to faith? How does it increase your trust in Jesus?

4. How powerful are the words of Jesus? Is that power still in His words?

5. How do we open the door to Jesus?

6. If we trust that Jesus hears us, how does that shape our daily living?

ELEVEN

SENSING THE FATHER

Psalm 8:3-5, 19:1-4, Matthew 5:14-16, Romans 1:19-20, 2 Timothy 3:15-17, Hebrews 4:12-13, 1 John 4:20-21

My dad died several years ago, but there are times when I especially sense his presence. When I look in the mirror, I see my dad. Every year when I was growing up, we took our vacation to the mountains. When I go to those mountains today, my dad is with me. Almost everything interested Dad. When I'm reading a book or visiting a museum or strolling through an antique shop, I think, *Dad would love this.* I especially feel dad near when I'm around those who knew him best. Then the stories and the memories flow. Dad is still with me.

What do I mean? Dad is not physically with me. He has gone to be with the Lord. I do not see a ghost of my dad. Since Dad is with God, he is alive, and someday, I will see him again in a resurrected body in a new heaven and earth. Even now, I sense his presence.

There are similarities between my sensing my dad and our sensing our heavenly Father. No, God is not dead, but we perceive the Father indirectly through creation, the Bible, and people. Though not a physical perception, it is real. Spiritually, our Father is nearer to us than the mom and dad we can see or once could see with our own eyes. The love that Father has for us is even greater than the deep affection we have from our parents.

SENSING THE FATHER IN CREATION

When God the Father called creation into existence, He repeatedly called it "good," even "very good" (Genesis 1:4, 10, 12, 18, 25, 31). Creation, though, is not the way God originally made it. Because humans sinned, the ground was cursed (3:17). The beauty of creation was disfigured.

That disfiguring is hard to believe as I look out at my garden on a spring morning. The trees are beginning to bud. The grass is turning green. The flowers are blooming with a panoply of colors. The sky is a bright blue with puffy, white clouds. All this overwhelms my senses, not just sight but the smell of new growth, the sound of birds, the impending taste of summer fruits, and the touch of the soil beneath my fingers.

There is beauty in the world. That beauty speaks loudly of a greater beauty. It tells of the One who made it all, the One who is beauty itself.

> The heavens proclaim the glory of God.
>   The skies display his craftsmanship.
> Day after day they continue to speak;
>   night after night they make him known.
> They speak without a sound or word;
>   their voice is never heard.

> Yet their message has gone throughout the earth,
>   and their words to all the world.
>
> PSALM 19:1-4

What do we mean when we look at the skies, the mountains, the sea, and the land and say, "That's beautiful"? Yes, we mean, "I like that," but we mean so much more. It's as if the glory of what we see fills us, leaving us without the words to express what we feel. We search for words. *Amazing. Majestic.* Even the overused, *Awesome.* What we see, hear, touch, smell, and taste overwhelms those senses. We catch a glimpse of a God who is good and true but also beautiful.

God the Father speaks through His creation. He says, "I am here. I made everything good for you. I am beyond your imagination. I love you infinitely." That voice speaks to all, even those who were not part of God's covenant people.

> They know the truth about God because he has made it obvious to them. For ever since the world was created, people have seen the earth and sky. Through everything God made, they can clearly see his invisible qualities — his eternal power and divine nature. So they have no excuse for not knowing God.
>
> ROMANS 1:19-20

Sadly, Paul goes on to say that those who should have known this glorious God refused to see or hear Him. They even made up their own gods. We can encounter the glories of creation and explain them in naturalistic ways, or we can bow in humility and gratitude to the Great Artisan who formed them.

We ourselves are His greatest work of art.

> When I look at the night sky and see the work of your fingers—
>> the moon and the stars you set in place—
> what are mere mortals that you should think about them,
>> human beings that you should care for them?
> Yet you made them only a little lower than God
>> and crowned them with glory and honor.
>
> PSALM 8:3-5

When the psalmist looked at the night sky, he was bewildered by how small he was. In our time, when we can look at the depths of the universe with powerful telescopes, we feel even smaller. When we think that our most advanced scientific instruments can only see a fraction of the universe, then we shrink even more. Humans are so insignificant, a flyspeck in the cosmos.

Our Creator says, "That's not true. I made you as the pinnacle of creation. Just lower than the angels." We will talk below about sensing God in other people. When we get a taste of the scope of God's creation, we experience Him with all our senses. We see, hear, touch, smell, and taste Him in the world around us. We know we are not small but great in his sight.

SENSING THE FATHER IN THE SCRIPTURES

We looked earlier at hearing God speak to us in the Bible. Let's explore that. The Father uses the Scriptures to shape us. God's Word gave us a new birth (James 1:18). "Your new life will last forever because it comes from the eternal, living word of God" (1 Peter 1:23). The Father sees who we truly are through that living Word.

> For the word of God is alive and powerful. It is sharper than the sharpest two-edged sword, cutting between soul and

> spirit, between joint and marrow. It exposes our innermost thoughts and desires. Nothing in all creation is hidden from God. Everything is naked and exposed before his eyes, and he is the one to whom we are accountable.
>
> HEBREWS 4:12-13

The picture here is not of us sharpening the sword to do battle with others. Bible study is not so much our mastering of the Scriptures. Instead, it is the Great Physician who uses the living scalpel of the Word to open our hearts to Him. Through His Word, God sees who we are, not what we pretend to be. In the Bible, we see God, and He sees us.

The Father uses the Scriptures to prepare us to do His will. Paul reminds Timothy of the power of the Word.

> You have been taught the holy Scriptures from childhood, and they have given you the wisdom to receive the salvation that comes by trusting in Christ Jesus. All Scripture is inspired by God and is useful to teach us what is true and to make us realize what is wrong in our lives. It corrects us when we are wrong and teaches us to do what is right. God uses it to prepare and equip his people to do every good work.
>
> 2 TIMOTHY 3:15-17

Scripture is inspired, literally in Greek, "God-breathed." The same Creator who breathed life into humans breathes life into the Bible. Many have argued over exactly how God inspires Scripture. The Bible does not tell us exactly *how*. This passage is more concerned with *why* God inspires Scripture. What does the Father do to us through the Bible? He corrects, teaches, prepares and equips. He gives His wisdom. Knowing the Bible is of no help if we do not let it mold us into the people of God.

Think of the diverse ways we sense God in the Bible. We see Him there, not just by seeing the words on a page but by letting those words sink into our hearts. We hear God in the Bible. We literally hear those words when others read or teach them to us, but we hear His voice in a deeper way. The Bible as a physical object is not sacred. It is not magic. It does not save us in itself. It points to One who saves. Holding the Bible in our hands, whether as a heavy, giant-print version or on our phones, gives us a tactile experience of God's Word. We touch the Bible, but more importantly, the Father touches us through it.

Ezekiel and John even tasted the Bible. A voice from heaven tells Ezekiel to eat a scroll. He does and finds it tastes sweet (Ezekiel 3:1-3). A similar voice tells John to do the same. He eats a scroll that tastes sweet in his mouth but turns sour in his stomach (Revelation 10:10). I'm not suggesting we eat our Bibles, but these stories do raise the question, "Does the Bible taste good to you?" Do we taste it often enough? Can we taste the goodness of God in our Bible study?

SENSING THE FATHER THROUGH OTHERS

One place we sense God is through other people. That isn't surprising since the Creator made humans in His image (Genesis 1:26). What does that mean? It does not mean we are God, but that we look like Him. I am not my dad, but if you saw picture of us together, you would see the resemblance. When we look at those around us, we get a glimpse of the Father.

Really? The people I'm around don't often act or look like God. It's true we live in a fallen world, but the worst person you can imagine bears the image of God. It may be a distorted image, but it is still there. What we must do is try to see the goodness of God in them. Perhaps this is what Paul meant when he said he "stopped evaluating others from a human point of view" (2 Corinthians 5:16). When we see people through the eyes of Christ, we see the likeness of God.

Doing that is difficult. We are happy to see the Father who loves us, the Son who saved us, and the Spirit who lives in us. We love God but are not so sure about people who are so difficult to love, some of whom are our fellow church members. We think we can sense God better if we don't have to deal with others. God will not allow that choice.

> If someone says, "I love God," but hates a fellow believer, that person is a liar; for if we don't love people we can see, how can we love God, whom we cannot see? And he has given us this command: Those who love God must also love their fellow believers.
>
> 1 JOHN 4:20-21

We not only see God in our brothers and sisters in Christ, but we also show our love for God by loving them. We show that love at all times, but it should be particularly visible when we assemble together for worship and prayer. Jesus said, "I also tell you this: If two of you agree here on earth concerning anything you ask, my Father in heaven will do it for you. For where two or three gather together as my followers, I am there among them" (Matthew 18:19-20). Praying and worshiping together involves all our senses. There we perceive that Jesus, the Father, and the Spirit are among us.

We sense God in others. We also are to show them the Father by our actions.

> "You are the light of the world — like a city on a hilltop that cannot be hidden. No one lights a lamp and then puts it

under a basket. Instead, a lamp is placed on a stand, where it gives light to everyone in the house. In the same way, let your good deeds shine out for all to see, so that everyone will praise your heavenly Father."

MATTHEW 5:14-16

There are many around us who are lost in every sense of the word. They cannot find their way in life. They stumble from one pleasure to another not able to see where they are going. They listen to all kinds of distracting voices but cannot hear a word from God. They need the light of God. As we sense the love of the Father in so many ways, we must light the way for others to find Him.

QUESTIONS FOR REFLECTION

1. Where do you find beauty in your life?

2. Why did God make so much that is pleasing to our senses?

3. What does it mean that the Bible is inspired?

4. How does Scripture guide you each day?

5. Think of some people who showed the Father to you. How can you show your gratefulness for them?

6. How do we let our light shine for others to see God without looking as if we were better than they?

TWELVE

SENSING THE SON

John 14:13-14, 16:23-24, Romans 6:3-5, 8:34, Galatians 3:26-28, Hebrews 7:24-25, 10:19-22, 1 John 2:1, 3:2, Colossians 3:4

I recently had a conversation with a friend about the various places to which we had traveled. We found that we had visited many of the same national parks. We had even lived in the same city for a while, but not at the same time. That led us to share the experiences we each had seen and enjoyed in those places. That talk brought us closer to each other.

Even more delightful is to go on a trip with a friend. Then you get to encounter the sights, sounds, smells, and tastes through his senses, not just your own. Shared experiences make for special memories.

We have shared experiences with Jesus. Because He is a fellow human, He has the same senses that we do. As God in the flesh, He also shares experiences with the Father. By traveling with Jesus, by doing things with Him, we encounter the living God.

BAPTISM, SUPPER, ASSEMBLY

Certain actions connect us to Jesus. Chief among them is baptism.

> So in Christ Jesus you are all children of God through faith, for all of you who were baptized into Christ have clothed yourselves with Christ. There is neither Jew nor Gentile, neither slave nor free, nor is there male and female, for you are all one in Christ Jesus.
>
> GALATIANS 3:26-28, NIV

We are baptized into Christ. Can there be any closer relationship? Baptism changed our identity. We no longer see ourselves primarily as part of a nationality, economic group, or even gender. We see ourselves as one with Jesus.

Baptized into Christ means we share in the experience of the baptism of Jesus. When Jesus was baptized, He felt the water, He saw the Spirit descend, and He heard the voice from heaven say, "This is my Son, whom I love; with him I am well pleased" (Matthew 3:17, NIV). The same things happened at our baptism. We felt the water that washed away our sins (Acts 22:16). We may not have seen a dove descend, but through eyes of faith, we did see the Spirit descend. By faith, we heard the voice of God call His beloved child.

This is more than merely following the example of Jesus by being baptized. In baptism, there is an intimate and dynamic union between us and Jesus. We are baptized *with* Him. We are baptized *into* Him. We share in His baptism but also in His death and resurrection. We join Jesus on the cross and in the empty tomb.

> Or have you forgotten that when we were joined with Christ Jesus in baptism, we joined him in his death? For we died

> and were buried with Christ by baptism. And just as Christ was raised from the dead by the glorious power of the Father, now we also may live new lives.
>
> Since we have been united with him in his death, we will also be raised to life as he was.
>
> ROMANS 6:3-5

Jesus calls us to take up the cross and follow Him (Mark 8:34). Baptism is our first step in carrying the cross. We are crucified with Christ. This means we suffer with Jesus. It also means our old self died with Him: "We know that our old sinful selves were crucified with Christ so that sin might lose its power in our lives. We are no longer slaves to sin" (Romans 6:6). At baptism, sin loses its power over us. Dead people don't sin. Remember how you felt when you were raised from the waters of baptism. Remember how clean you felt from your sins. That sense of being washed and clean is with us every moment through the blood of Christ (1 John 1:7).

Christians should have no fear of death because we already died. Been there, done that. We died in baptism. Death was not the last word for Jesus. It is not the last word for us. We also are raised from the waters of baptism as Jesus was raised from the dead. That means a new life now. It also means that our bodies will be raised with His at the last day (Romans 8:11). It's hard to imagine how Jesus felt at this resurrection. His senses came back to life. What's more, His resurrected body likely had a deeper way of perceiving the world through His senses. One day, our bodies will share those new senses.

The Bible describes the inseparable intimacy we have with Jesus in baptism as "putting on Christ" (Galatians 3:27, Ephesians 4:24, Colossians 3:10). What is closer to us than our clothes? Clothes touch us. We feel them, see them, and smell them. So Jesus is always near us. He is on us. When others see us, they first notice what we are wearing. Now they see Jesus on us.

We sense Jesus in baptism. We also sense Him in the Lord's Supper. We looked at how we taste Jesus in an earlier chapter, but let's briefly review. Jesus calls Himself the bread of life (John 6:32-58). By eating the bread at the Supper, we have the life of Jesus in us. When we eat the bread and drink from the cup, we share in the body and blood of Jesus (1 Corinthians 10:16). The Lord's Supper is a memorial, but it is a deeper experience than simply remembering the death of Jesus. Jesus could have just said, "Remember me." Instead, He gave us sensory reminders of His death — bread and wine we can touch, smell, and taste. He could have said, "These represent my body." That is not what He said. His words were, "This is my body. This is my blood." In the Supper, as in baptism, Jesus is fully present with us.

We also sense Jesus when we meet with other Christians. "For where two or three gather together as my followers, I am there among them" (Matthew 18:20). When we gather as a church, we see, hear, touch, and smell our fellow Christians, the body of Christ. Jesus sits beside us, sings with us, listens with us, and prays with us.

PRAYER

Jesus prayed. Have you ever thought about the significance of that? The eternal Son of God felt the need to pray. After He fed the 5,000, He needed to get away from the crowd to be alone with His Father. He dismissed the disciples and the crowd and spent most of the night by Himself in prayer. (Matthew 14:22-23). Another time, after a long day of healing, Jesus rose early to be by Himself to pray (Mark 1:35). Whether late after everyone was asleep or early before they were awake, Jesus made time to pray. This was a discipline, a regular practice for Jesus (Luke 5:15-16).

Jesus also prayed at the turning points in His life. He prayed at His baptism (Luke 3:21). He spent all night in prayer before choosing the apostles (Luke 6:12-13). Once, when He was praying with His disciples, He asked them who they thought He was. Peter answered, "You are the Messiah" (Luke 9:18-20). Jesus is praying with Peter, James, and John when He is transfigured before them, and they see Him in His glory (Luke 9:28-31). Jesus prays before He raises Lazarus from the dead (John 11:41-44). Daily, and in the crises of life, Jesus prayed.

And He prayed with His body. He prayed with His eyes lifted to heaven (John 11:41, 17:1). He knelt in prayer (Luke 22:41). He fell on His face in prayer (Matthew 26:39). While praying in Gethsemane, His sweat became blood (Luke 22:44). He cried in prayer (Hebrews 5:7). Jesus prayed with all His senses. He heard His own voice and the voice of the Father. He lifted His eyes to see God in heaven. He felt the ground under His knees. He tasted His own tears.

That same Jesus now prays with us. He is our great High Priest who intercedes for us.

> But because Jesus lives forever, his priesthood lasts forever. Therefore he is able, once and forever, to save those who come to God through him. He lives forever to intercede with God on their behalf.
>
> HEBREWS 7:24-25

The function of a priest is to stand between humans and God. Since Jesus is both God and human, He is the perfect High Priest. The priest brings the offerings of the people to the Lord.

So Jesus brings our requests to God: "While Jesus was here on earth, he offered prayers and pleadings, with a loud cry and tears, to the one who could rescue him from death. And God heard his prayers because of his deep reverence for God" (Hebrews 5:7). He continues to plead, not for Himself, but for us.

> My dear children, I am writing this to you so that you will not sin. But if anyone does sin, we have an advocate who pleads our case before the Father. He is Jesus Christ, the one who is truly righteous.
>
> 1 JOHN 2:1

> Who then will condemn us? No one — for Christ Jesus died for us and was raised to life for us, and he is sitting in the place of honor at God's right hand, pleading for us.
>
> ROMANS 8:34

The picture here is of a defense attorney who pleads our case before the Great Judge. The Father will not condemn us because the One who pleads for us is the One who paid the debt we owe.

So when we pray, we sense the presence of Jesus praying with us and praying for us. We remind ourselves of that by praying, "in Jesus' name." Many of us end our prayers with those words. They mean more than, "The prayer is ended." They mean our prayers are His and His prayers ours. And those words come with an amazing promise.

> You can ask for anything in my name, and I will do it, so that the Son can bring glory to the Father. Yes, ask me for anything in my name, and I will do it!
>
> JOHN 14:13-14

> At that time you won't need to ask me for anything. I tell you the truth, you will ask the Father directly, and he will grant your request because you use my name. You haven't done this before. Ask, using my name, and you will receive, and you will have abundant joy.
>
> JOHN 16:23-24

Jesus will give us anything we ask for in His name. Anything? Yes, because when we pray in the name of Jesus, we always make the request of the Father that Jesus made in the Garden, "Yet I want your will to be done, not mine" (Matthew 26:39).

What an amazing privilege it is to come before God in prayer! We enter the very throne room of the Almighty with boldness, because we never enter alone. Jesus is with us. We enter as those who are baptized with Jesus, who eat the bread of life, and who pray with our great High Priest. All our senses are filled with abundant joy.

> And so, dear brothers and sisters, we can boldly enter heaven's Most Holy Place because of the blood of Jesus. By his death, Jesus opened a new and life-giving way through the curtain into the Most Holy Place. And since we have a great High Priest who rules over God's house, let us go right into the presence of God with sincere hearts fully trusting him. For our guilty consciences have been sprinkled with Christ's blood to make us clean, and our bodies have been washed with pure water.
>
> HEBREWS 10:19-22

GLORY

With all our senses we share in the life of Jesus. We are one with Him in baptism, the Lord's Supper, assembly, and prayer. But that is only a taste of what is to come. With heightened and renewed senses, we will be one with Jesus in the new heaven and earth. We will not only see His glory, but we will share in it.

> Dear friends, we are already God's children, but he has not yet shown us what we will be like when Christ appears. But we do know that we will be like him, for we will see him as he really is.
>
> 1 JOHN 3:2

> And when Christ, who is your life, is revealed to the whole world, you will share in all his glory.
>
> COLOSSIANS 3:4

Perhaps you remember the song written by Bart Millard of the group Mercy Me, "I Can Only Imagine." Those words invited us to imagine the glory of Jesus that we will share. We cannot imagine it. Yet even now we have a sense of the eternal Presence of the Son of God.

Christianity is an embodied faith. God took on a body. The body of Jesus could smell, see, touch, taste, and hear. We sense Jesus with our bodies in the waters of baptism, in the bread and wine, and in our fellow believers. One day, we will sense Him in our resurrected bodies. May that day be soon!

QUESTIONS FOR REFLECTION

1. What did Jesus feel at His baptism? What did you feel at your baptism?

2. How do we sense Jesus in our fellow Christians?

3. Why do we end our prayers, "In Jesus' Name"? What does that mean?

4. What does it mean to pray, "God's will be done"? When was the last time you had trouble accepting God's will?

5. How are all our senses involved in prayer?

6. Imagine with all your senses what it will be like when we share the glory of Jesus. What will we feel?

THIRTEEN
SENSING THE SPIRIT

Joel 2:28-29, John 14:17-18, 23, Romans 15:16, Galatians 5:22-25, 1 Corinthians 2:13-14, 6:19-20, 1 Peter 1:2, 2 Peter 1:20-21

We perceive the Father and the Son through our senses. That seems harder to understand when it comes to the Spirit. The flesh and blood Jesus had the five senses we have. Spirits do not have bodies. Yet we rightly sense God the Father, even though Jesus says, "God is Spirit" (John 4:24). Why does the Holy Spirit seem more mysterious than the Father and the Son?

Perhaps because older Bible versions spoke of the "Holy Ghost." That was a fine translation in its day, but "Ghost" makes us think of what is insubstantial and unreal. Spirit can also sound that way. Although we rightly can contrast the spiritual with the physical, we should never contrast spiritual with real. The Spirit does not have a body, but He is no ghostly presence. He is as genuinely God as the Father and the Son.

RECEIVING THE SPIRIT

The Spirit, like the Father, has no physical body, but it enters into physical bodies to give them power to serve God. People can see and hear when that happens.

For example, in the Old Testament, the Spirit comes upon Joshua (Numbers 27:18), Othniel (Judges 3:10), Gideon (Judges 6:34), Samson (Judges 13:25; 14:6), and Saul (1 Samuel 10:9, 10). People could see the Spirit in Joshua, Othniel and Gideon, through their powerful leadership in battle. Samson's powerful touch came through the Spirit. The Spirit causes Saul to prophesy in such a dramatically visible way that the people comment on it. David (2 Samuel 23:2), Ezekiel (Ezekiel 2:2), and others also prophecy when the Spirit comes upon them.

But not all of God's people receive the Spirit in the Old Testament, although there is hope that someday they will. When Moses and 70 elders receive the Spirit, Moses says, "I wish that all the LORD's people were prophets and that the LORD would put his Spirit upon them all!" (Numbers 11:29). God promises to restore Israel after their exile and put a new heart in them through the Spirit (Ezekiel 36:26-27). God tells Joel:

> "Then, after doing all those things,
>   I will pour out my Spirit upon all people.
> Your sons and daughters will prophesy.
>   Your old men will dream dreams,
>   and your young men will see visions.
> In those days I will pour out my Spirit
>   even on servants — men and women alike."
>
> JOEL 2:28-29

On the day of Pentecost after the resurrection of Jesus, the Holy Spirit comes upon the disciples. Those around them see flames on their heads and hear them speak in other languages. When they wonder what it all means, Peter says the words of Joel have come to pass. The Spirit is available to all who repent and are baptized in the name of Jesus (Acts 2:1-38).

When Paul meets followers of Jesus who have never heard of the Holy Spirit, he knows something isn't quite right with their baptism. Finding they had been baptized by John the Baptist, he told them of baptism in the name of Jesus. After they are baptized in Jesus' name, they receive the Spirit and speak in tongues and prophesy (Acts 19:1-7).

We receive the Spirit at baptism. That does not mean that baptism contains the Spirit. We cannot control the Spirit through baptism. God gives the Spirit however and whenever God wills. When Peter preaches to Cornelius and his family, they receive the Spirit and speak in tongues before they are baptized (Acts 10:44-48).

But usually the Spirit comes at baptism. Jesus also received the Spirit at His baptism. How can that be? Did not the Son of God already have the Holy Spirit? Of course, He did! But He also needed the power of the Spirit to do His ministry of healing and teaching. The Spirit also empowers us for service.

How do we know we received the Spirit at baptism? In three of the cases above, those who were baptized spoke in tongues. Yet not all who are baptized speak in tongues (1 Corinthians 12:30). Is tongue-speaking the only sign of the Spirit? No. As we will see, there are many signs of the Spirit's presence in our lives. We must look and listen for the work of the Spirit.

HEARING THE SPIRIT

The Spirit speaks to us in Scripture. We saw how He spoke to the prophets.

> Above all, you must realize that no prophecy in Scripture ever came from the prophet's own understanding, or from human initiative. No, those prophets were moved by the Holy Spirit, and they spoke from God.
>
> 2 PETER 1:20-21

God breathed out the Scriptures through the Spirit. That's why the Bible refers to the Spirit speaking (Hebrews 3:7, 10:15). We should listen to the Spirit speak. "Anyone with ears to hear must listen to the Spirit and understand what he is saying to the churches" (Revelation 2:7,11, 17, 29, 3:6, 13, 22).

And the Spirit helps us hear and understand.

> When we tell you these things, we do not use words that come from human wisdom. Instead, we speak words given to us by the Spirit, using the Spirit's words to explain spiritual truths. But people who aren't spiritual can't receive these truths from God's Spirit. It all sounds foolish to them and they can't understand it, for only those who are spiritual can understand what the Spirit means.
>
> 1 CORINTHIANS 2:13-14

We read the Bible with our eyes and hear it with our ears. The Spirit speaks through the Bible. What's more, the Spirit in us gives us understanding of what we read and hear. He empowers us to listen and obey. That's why Paul says, "I have not stopped thanking God for you. I pray for you constantly, asking God, the glorious Father of our Lord Jesus Christ, to give you spiritual wisdom and insight so that you might grow in your knowledge of God" (Ephesians 1:16-17).

THE SPIRIT IN US

The Spirit speaks in the Bible, and He also speaks in us. That isn't surprising because the Spirit lives in us.

> Don't you realize that your body is the temple of the Holy Spirit, who lives in you and was given to you by God? You do not belong to yourself, for God bought you with a high price. So you must honor God with your body.
>
> 1 CORINTHIANS 6:19-20

As Spirit, God has no body. He became flesh in the body of Jesus. Now through the Holy Spirit, God is embodied in each of us that Jesus bought with His blood. The Spirit also lives in the church, the body of Christ (Ephesians 2:21-22). That means that God the Spirit enters the world through our five senses.

This embodied Spirit does so much in us and through us. Just to give a few examples.

- **The Spirit assures us that we belong to God.**
  "So you have not received a spirit that makes you fearful slaves. Instead, you received God's Spirit when he adopted you as his own children. Now we call him, "Abba, Father." For his Spirit joins with our spirit to affirm that we are God's children" (Romans 8:15-16).
- **He gives us confidence and hope.**
  "I pray that God, the source of hope, will fill you completely with joy and peace because you trust in him. Then you will overflow with confident hope through the power of the Holy Spirit" (Romans 15:13, see also Ephesians 3:16, 2 Timothy 1:7).

- **He helps us pray.**

  "And the Holy Spirit helps us in our weakness. For example, we don't know what God wants us to pray for. But the Holy Spirit prays for us with groanings that cannot be expressed in words. And the Father who knows all hearts knows what the Spirit is saying, for the Spirit pleads for us believers in harmony with God's own will" (Romans 8:26-27, see also Ephesians 6:18, Jude 20).

- **He gives gifts for the benefit of the entire church.**

  "A spiritual gift is given to each of us so we can help each other" (1 Corinthians 12:7, see also 1 Corinthians 12:1-31, Romans 12:4-8, 1 Peter 4:10-11).

- **He gives power and direction for mission.**

  "One day as these men were worshiping the Lord and fasting, the Holy Spirit said, 'Appoint Barnabas and Saul for the special work to which I have called them.' So after more fasting and prayer, the men laid their hands on them and sent them on their way" (Acts 13:2-3, see also Acts 1:8, 8:29, 16:6).

THE HOLY SPIRIT MAKES US HOLY

The primary work of the Spirit in us is to make us like God. The character of God is called holiness. "You must be holy because I, the LORD your God, am holy" (Leviticus 19:2, quoted in 1 Peter 1:16).

What does it mean that God is holy? Think of everything God is. God is powerful and majestic. God is good and pure. God is compassionate and merciful. God is faithful and dependable. We can summarize all the ways we describe God by this one word, *Holy*.

The word *holy*, however, does not communicate well in our culture. If we hear someone described as holy, we immediately think them a prideful hypocrite, one who thinks they are holier than others. Perhaps, we should say *godly* instead of *holy*. The Spirit is transforming us into the character of God. He makes us godly.

> I bring you the Good News so that I might present you as an acceptable offering to God, made holy by the Holy Spirit.
>
> ROMANS 15:16

> God the Father knew you and chose you long ago, and his Spirit has made you holy. As a result, you have obeyed him and have been cleansed by the blood of Jesus Christ.
>
> 1 PETER 1:2

Holy is still the word we find in most Bible versions. Most versions use vastly different English words to translate words that have the same root in Greek — *holy*, *sanctify*, and *saint*. To get a feel for what the Spirit does in us, we might say the Holy Spirit holifies (sanctifies) us so that we may be holy people (saints).

How does the Spirit do this? He does it through all the ways we have studied in this book, ways that we sense God and God senses us. He does it through Bible study, prayer, baptism, the Lord's Supper, and assembly. He also does it at every moment by living in us. There is a mysterious process here that the Bible describes as producing fruit.

> But the Holy Spirit produces this kind of fruit in our lives: love, joy, peace, patience, kindness, goodness, faithfulness,

> gentleness, and self-control. There is no law against these things!
>
> Those who belong to Christ Jesus have nailed the passions and desires of their sinful nature to his cross and crucified them there. Since we are living by the Spirit, let us follow the Spirit's leading in every part of our lives.
>
> GALATIANS 5:22-25

We can touch, smell, see, and taste fruit. We can do the same with the fruit of the Spirit in our lives and the lives of other Christians. These fruits are not natural human goodness. They are the supernatural work of God in us.

As you read this book, you may have thought, *Why are we talking about sensing God?* The idea of knowing God through our senses may even have struck you as sacrilegious. Who can get close enough to see, hear, smell, touch, and taste God?

No one can. The great news is that God has come near to us, so close that we can say Father, Son and Spirit make their home with us. Jesus promises that to His disciples.

> He is the Holy Spirit, who leads into all truth. The world cannot receive him, because it isn't looking for him and doesn't recognize him. But you know him, because he lives with you now and later will be in you. No, I will not abandon you as orphans — I will come to you.
>
> All who love me will do what I say. My Father will love them, and we will come and make our home with each of them.
>
> JOHN 14:17-18, 23

Father, Son, and Spirit make their home with us. They live in our bodies through the Spirit. May God hasten the day when we are at home with Them forever.

QUESTIONS FOR REFLECTION

1. Has your church talked too little or too much about the Holy Spirit? What is the reason for that?

2. How did the Spirit work in the Old Testament?

3. Did you know you received the Spirit at your baptism? If so, how did that help you? If not, how would it have helped?

4. How do we listen to the Spirit?

5. Of all the ways the Spirit works in our lives, which impacts you the most? Why?

6. How has this study helped you sense God in your life?

www.ingramcontent.com/pod-product-compliance
Lightning Source LLC
Chambersburg PA
CBHW070201100426
42743CB00013B/2996